What the L?

ALSO BY KATE CLINTON

Don't Get Me Started

What the L?

KATE CLINTON

CARROLL & GRAF PUBLISHERS

NEW YORK

WHAT THE L?

Carroll & Graf Publishers
An Imprint of Avalon Publishing Group Inc.
245 West 17th Street
New York, NY 10011

AVALON
publishing group incorporated

First Carroll & Graf edition 2005

Many of these articles have appeared in *The Advocate* and *The Progressive*, with "Making Light" first being published in *Trivia*.

Library of Congress Cataloging-in-Publication Data is available.

ISBN: 0-7867-1544-8

Printed in the United States of America
Interior design by Jamie McNeely
Distributed by Publishers Group West

For Urvashi Vaid,
my culture war bride

What the L?

CONTENTS

My Malformative Years

Mad Vow Disease

Afterword

ACKNOWLEDGMENT

I WOULD LIKE TO THANK Matt Rothschild at *The Progressive* and Judy Wieder and Anne Stockwell at *The Advocate* for providing me with the opportunity to write many of the columns that comprise this book.

INTRODUCTION

"IT'S OVER."

A huge cheer went up, gay men and lesbians leapt up from their chairs whooping, waving, then throwing their napkins up in the air. With little prompting from me, we all sang, "Happy Days are Here Again," or at least the four lines we all knew of that old song.

It was January, 1993, Washington DC, and I was emceeing a big raucous dinner sponsored by several national Gay Lesbian Bisexual Transgender organizations, on the eve of the first inauguration of Bill Clinton. I stood up to the microphone. Instead of "It's over," I had planned to say, "Welcome, and thank you all for coming out."

The spontaneous joy of the moment was in direct proportion to the twelve years of misery we had just lived through. The hugging, kissing, laughing, crying and partying felt like the V-J and V-E Day World War II ending celebrations my parents had described.

The next night, after Clinton's swearing in, I emceed more of the rejoicing at the Triangle Ball. The hotel ballroom was hot, loud and packed with men in tuxedoes festively accessorized for the occasion with rainbow cummerbunds and women in dresses laden with sequins that looked like they had been bought by the pound. Or maybe it was men in dresses, women in tuxes.

My outfit was a gold lame jacket over a silver shirt. On my head I had tied a black and glittering gold scarf. In pictures of that night, my head looks like a high end bundt cake with spiky hair exploding out the top. I could claim a fashion statement, but in reality, the scarf was to keep my head from exploding.

After eight years of Reagan, who had only once in those years uttered the word AIDS as it cut a wide swathe through our friends, and four years of a George Bush who at the time needed no other identifying numerals, we were stunned to have a president who had reached out to the gay community during his campaign and seemed able to say gay and lesbian often and without any accompanying lip-curling distaste. It was very disorienting. And eventually disappointing.

Saying that the Clinton years were disappointing is a lot like saying, "I'm so disappointed in the patriarchy." Besides passing NAFTA, failing to reform or begin to reform healthcare, and his triangulating three-ways, his

"Don't Ask; Don't Tell" solution to the problem [for straight people] of gays in the military was no solution at all. His signing of the Defense of Marriage Act seemed to be his way of saving marriage from himself.

Despite the frustrations, the Clinton years were still markedly more welcoming than the previous Reagan/Bush lockout, so gay people came out in droves: professional and amateur gays, Log Cabin Republicans and Stonewall Democrats, rodeo riders, gay cruisers, circuit party gays, gay choraliers, gay ministers, equal-sign gays, openly closeted, sporty, sexy, political and apolitical, academic and redneck, old and young, no, I mean really young, gay people all came out.

Faster than you can say "niche market," businesses realized they could make money on this newly visible gay population. The gay movement began an affair with the corporate America and, have your rainbow credit cards handy, the gay market was opened for business. On TV, in movies, and in the news, the love that dared not speak its name wouldn't shut up about it already. During the Clinton impeachment, in poll after poll, the American people inadvertently validated employment nondiscrimination claims, when they said they didn't care what he did in the bedroom, or even in the copy room, as long as he did his job. We were at peace; there were surpluses.

What the L happened?

This essay collection chronicles what happened to lots of Ls: lesbians, liberals, leftists, lawyers, Ellen, lifestylists, leaders, lords, liars, lapsed Catholics, lovers and losers in the reign of W. Of course the seeds of many losses were sown in BC, the Bill Clinton years: corporate scandals, economic policies that led to a politics of resentment; gay rights bills stalled in state legislatures; increased antigay violence; and Clinton's self-serving tack to the right that killed many a progressive reform. Those were the good old days.

This collection is written from the perspective of, to paraphrase a certain former governor of New Jersey, a Lesbian American. Moi. Pardon my freedom. I've been both for quite some time now. Being a lesbian is one of the most interesting things I have ever chosen to do. I love my country and I hate what's happening.

I mean "What the L?" not in a pessimistic, shocked and awed, bug-eyed, incredulous, leaving-the-country, head-shakingly sad, somebody-always-ends-up-in-fears recitation of a slimily slicked series of unfortunate current events tone, but rather, in a buoyant, smart-ass, get-a-load-of-this, relentlessly optimistic, might-as-well-live "What the L?" tone. A leap of faith, if you will. And I will.

How the L did we get lulled into thinking it was over? What the L do we do to make sure it doesn't happen again? How the L are we going to survive? In my personal home-land terrorist survival kit, in addition to the canned goods, some Clarins anti-wrinkle gravity creams and of course batteries, I have made sure there has always been a good stock of L-rations, i.e., laughter.

Humor has taken quite a hit lately—from the preemptively self-deprecating, shoulder-bouncing, heh-heh-heh single entendred, nicknaming beevis Bush humor; to the big time derisively side-mouthed, butthead Cheney sarcasm; to the uncertain irony after September 11th; to the new p.c. of patriotic censorship; to the people against smiling fundamentalists; to the passively silent L.O.L. of forwarded cyber-humor lists; to the elimination humor of the last comic standing; to the gut-busters at FAUX news. With the exception of the writing of Molly Ivins and the first fifteen minutes of the Daily Show with Jon Stewart, comedy has not been pretty. Or very funny.

But I believe humor will get us through.

For a long time I have claimed a lot for humor. [see "Making Light" Afterword]. Why the L stop now? I am a faith-based comic. In addition to the frivolous, salutary pleasure of laughing, I believe in the power of laughter to subvert authority and promote democracy. Laughter takes the tyranny of the lies we are told and told and told and it blows them apart. I espouse humor activism. Sometimes when I am sitting in lectures or debates, eavesdropping on or engaging in conversation in which I am forced to listen to huge steaming piles of lying illogic, I try not to go silent but to be a witness for truth. I laugh. I snort. Really hoot and say, "That's so funny . . . oh, you mean it." The laugh, with perhaps a satisfying but not mandatory dishy two-snap dismissal, destroys the fragile edifice of credibility holding up the story and messes with the confidence of the story-teller. Although there is a reckless relief in the release of laughter, it is not dissolute. It powers speech, a call to action and with it, a demand for change.

Because, turns out, like that mission accomplished thing, it is so not over.

FEBRUARY 2005

DOING A W-TAKE

●   ●   ●

The Clinton years were like being on comedy cruise control—prosperity, peace, sex scandals. Ho hum. Since the junta/coup/selection of 2000, it is as if the muse has been shouting, "You want material? I'll give you material!" It is an effort to keep up. To quote President Rain Man in the debates, "It's a hard job." I could not make this stuff up. I should write in italics, so you would have to read at a quizzical, head-tilted angle. What is made up— from pooling your tax rebate checks to managing your anger; from starting impeachment proceedings to dressing for surveillance; from marching for the hormoneland to dumping Slimfast in the harbor—is an attempt to make the best of a bad situation. What has been good for me, has been bad for us.

The Dust Bin
of History

SILLY ME. BUSH WAS ELECTED. War is the answer. A little torture is a good thing. Ditto racial profiling. I've got to learn to kick back and enjoy this White House effect. What was I thinking? What's that sound I hear? The Constitution being shredded? Whoopee! Confetti!

Of course I'm bitter that I was not offered the USO gig to entertain the troops at holiday time. No, that went to "the new Bob Hope," Wayne Newton. Unless there is an elite troop of altacockers special forces in Afghanistan we don't know about, which would be brilliant and unexpected, I would think that 'N Sync, Missy Misdemeanor Eliot, or Britney Spears would be a better choice. And I was just getting over my hurt feelings about not being asked to open for the Pope in his recent tour of Grease.

Since 9–11, I have been doing my own version of a USO

tour performing throughout the country. Did I already mention I love my country? When I leave the house, on a road trip or even on an errand, my own strict Dress for Success code has been replaced by Dress for Surveillance. You like to look your best for the cameras. When I was first searched at airport security, I actually felt relieved they were surveilling the less obvious suspects, larger older white gals like myself. After my fourth random wanding [not in the Harry Potter sense] from a lovely woman at O'Hare, I learned a new meaning of heightened state of alert.

And the troops are traumatized. At the beginning of every show, I have always thanked people for coming out, implying out of the closet. Now I mean out of the house. Since the polarized red/blue presidential selection process last November, I have found it harder to come out as a justice-loving progressive than as a lesbian. In the summer, before the WTC attacks, [did I already mention I loathed them?] people were nervous during the Bush bash section of my show. I pretended those who got up to leave had small bladders or had to have a smoke.

After 9–11, I was asked to appear at a Women's Breakfast the day before the almost overlooked NYC Democratic mayoral runoff. It was a powerfully diverse gathering of women—African-American, Asian-American, Latina, labor, political, organizers, activists. I was proud to be there and remarked that it was such a relief to be among women after days of watching men talking to other men about men, only men. The men had not yet picked up and played the convenient "we are freeing the Afghan women oppressed under the Taliban" card.

In a throwaway line, I referred to George Bin Bush. "Bin" as in "son of." The women in the audience did not bat an eye. But some reporter for the *New York Post* there picked it up, challenged the Ferrer people with it, and printed it the next day. My manager called me, frantic from phone threats, and my website was flamed with e-threats. Now I know what it takes to get in the *Post*.

No telling, if my remarks have already gotten me onto the list of offending comments compiled by Lon Cheney's "Committee to Protect American Civilization," not to be confused with "The Ministry for the Promotion of Virtue and Prevention of Vice." That's Bill Bennett. Cheney runs the Committee out of the secure and undisclosed bunker she shares with her husband, the Veep. It's a duck blind in Eastern PA. Todd Gitlin, professor at NYU, is on the list for the highly inflammatory statement, "There is lot of skepticism about America's policy of going to war." Sometimes I like to imagine Tipper Gore getting away with a committee like that.

Now I find myself approaching political material in my shows much as I approached the Golden Gate Bridge that day on tour when Gray Davis warned of possible, highly probable terrorist attacks. I take a deep breath and floor it.

(2001)

The Rush to Crown George Duh

IF I HAD A DOLLAR for each time someone has said to me, "You must be having a great time with all this material," referring to the unpleasantness in Florida, I would have at least $200. No, wait, after a full and fair recount, it's $203.47.

To paraphrase the Queen, it's been a *tempus horribilis*. Sure, sure, while others returned to work, my day job forced me to watch, read, listen, and click through the most nauseating pile of pookie since a protracted summer garbage strike in New York City. (That last analogy was my homage to the loopy late-night work of Dan Rather.)

Despite a lifelong commitment to nonviolence, my thoughts turned less toward humor and more toward homicide. As the Pretenders unearth more cadaverous

white men for The Nightly News of the Living Dead—
Marlin Fitzwater Lives!—one thing you can conclude is that
Republicans have mastered the secrets of cryogenics.

If you knew what I have fantasized doing to Jim Baker
and his hair plugs, for starters, you would be shocked. Perhaps not.

Instead of writing witty, sophisticated bons mots, I
found myself screaming adult things like "Liar, liar, pants
on fire" at anyone on Fox "We Will Decide Who's President" News. I find no solace in the Weather Channel
because Florida still dangles there.

As a fourth- or fifth-string pundit on CNN and
MSNBC, I have been called in several times to "give us
some humor" in the last two or three minutes of a so-called
news hour. Networks went through so many guest commentators they had to pass emergency hygiene guidelines
for the proper care and cleaning of earpieces.

As I sat in the guest chair and watched the clock tick down
to the fifty-seventh minute of the hour because someone
could not stop blathering on about the legitimacy of the
Banana Republicans, I considered telling Myles O'Brien
that I was spending an unnatural amount of time in bed with
Greta Van Susteren. But then I fantasized about pressing my
face into the camera and screaming, "Death to the corporate
media conglomerates! Jeb Bush had an affair with
Katherine Harris!! Rupert Murdoch is the Antichrist!"

One of the reasons we were told we had to rush to crown
George Duh is that we were the laughingstock of the world.
Oh, like that's something new. The only difference is that
whereas before our arrogance only merited a British tut

tut, a French eye roll, or a Serbian smirk, now there is open guffawing. And remember what Duh said in the so-called debates: Africa just doesn't count.

Of course, the linguistic possibilities of "Bush and Dick" would be enough for me to put it on comedy cruise control for the next four years. It's important to turn crises into opportunities and until the time I find some humor in all this, I have taken my $203.47 and preemptively formed The Permanent Standing Committee to Impeach Bush (TPSCTIB). Those who join from Florida get bonus double miles. It is modeled after the The Permanent Republican Committee of Sore Losers to Impeach Clinton that believed the presidency is a government entitlement program for Republicans and are still really steamed by the impertinent election of Bill Clinton.

Send any scurrilous personal Duh details, unverified Bush brushes, cockamamie conspiracy theories, or innuendos to TPSCTIB at kate@kateclinton.com and we will assign our own relentless Starr Chamber investigator to verify your claim, weeks after we post it. Remember, there is no shelf life to a really juicy bit.

Please note: TPSCTIB will not accept any of those dire e-lists of terrible things about Texas under Governor Duh. They didn't scare anyone. The opposite proved true: He's horrible. We can prove it. Let's elect him. Poor Molly Ivins, Shrub chronicler from way back, was like a modern-day Cassandra.

I've already got Bush Fatigue. Not the good kind.

(2001)

Pride?!
You're Kidding

AFTER ONE HUNDRED PLUS DAYS of Bush, has it only been that long? I find I have almost no room for pride. Rage. Not pride. I was raised Irish-Catholic and in my family, if you had an emotion, you went to your room. I suppose my therapist would be pleased with my progress. And if my therapist were Lorraine Bracco, therapist to the Sopranos, the other extended family in the news, I would want to please her.

I remember myself in the pre-GWB years as a fairly omni-emotional gal. Mad. Sad. Glad. I could do them all, multilayered and on a good day, simultaneously. Now I'm mono-emotional. I'm a huge energy-draining Rage Rover. I range from the very adult, snarky "I know you are, but what am I?" through the bitterly sarcastic "Oh, I bet you do, Bush Boy," to hop-spitting, vein-popping, homicidal fury, "Where's my Uzi, mother?" I'm a humvee of venom and I don't know where to park it.

It got so bad I had to call in the anger management people. They assured me that the anger I was experiencing was in direct proportion to the perversion of pride around me.

Pride is losing the popular vote by 500,000 or more and stealing the electoral votes from the state run by your brother, another of the pride of the Bush scions, and then acting as if you've got a popular mandate.

Pride is ramming a Japanese boat with your submarine and acting as if it was because you had a late lunch.

Pride is doing bombing practice on Vieques just because you can.

Pride is spying on another country, and getting caught and called on it. All China wanted was a phone call and an apology. We've all had exes like that. That would have been a great call, Prep in chief: 'Wazzzup? Crouching ti-ger, hidden li-on, wazzup?"

Pride is saying, "I wasn't there to welcome our spies home because I didn't want to disturb their personal tender moment," carried for hours on CNN. Meaning, "I've got four days of fishing at my bass pond in Crawford planned. No way I'm going."

Pride are those preemptive strikes of self-deprecating humor, which are nonetheless posited on a very large self. Whooee, lookit what I said. I'm an idiot. But I'm your idiot. And the dining press correspondents fall for it every time.

Then there's the whole pride of lyings. About who is really in charge, about the arsenic in the water, the salmonella in the meat, about who really benefits from the tax cut, about the estate tax, about the family DUIs, about the real plan for abortion and family planning funding, about those charter schools, about the drilling in Alaska, about workers rights, about the tokenathon for minorities, gays, women in the administration.

There's been so much yanking, it's a wonder he did away with those repetitive motion protections.

But I suppose anger is better than numbness. Although nothing can shut down my friends faster than my shrieking, "Did you hear what he said about Africa?" [Trick question, he never says anything about Africa.] They sigh and respond wearily, "I only watch 'The West Wing,'" as if it were their new spiritual practice of detachment.

I don't want to be annoying like some kind of Comic Cassandra, pointing out that these guys are wearing Stetsons and they're dragging a big wooden horse into the center of town. So I'm trying a new tact. Replace anger with faith. I'm a faith-based comic. Faith that this is the last blast of the blasted straight white guys. Faith that they won't take us all down with them when they go. It's dicey. They say pride goeth before the fall and at the rate they're going, it could go before summer time shares start.

So I'm forming my own church. The Kate Clinton Full Gospel Choir Urban Lesbian Swat Team and Marching Band. We hope to get some of those big federal funds. It will help to underwrite our Gay Pride Tour and the robes. Watch for us in a pride parade near you. We're right behind the horse.

(2001)

How I Spent My Summer Tax Rebate Check

THE FIRST WEEK IN JULY, I replaced the vacationing
Dick Cavett as narrator in *The Rocky Horror Show* on Broadway.
My old high school teaching skills came right back to me,
since it was my job to ride herd on a raucously interactive
audience who had grown up on midnight art house show-
ings of the movie.

Parents brought their young kids to the theater and on
ancient ritualized cues, yelled out the most scabrous things
at me, at the cast. Their children sat gape mouthed at their
parental units spewing obscenities, forbidden to them.
Brad. Asshole! Janet. Slut!

It was, in an airtight, uptight first world, wonderfully,
riotously transgressive. I encourage people to continue
the tradition, and give a shout out whenever they hear

the names of George or Dick or Rummy or any of the other horrors ranged before us. And I mean no insult to assholes.

All of July, I breathlessly awaited the debut of the "new" CNN. Formerly Clinton Nook News, now Conduit [slut!] the get-to-the-point nutwork proclaimed desperately, "We're doing things different!" Forgoing adverbs? Muzzling Tucker [asshole!] Carlson? Doing some actual investigative journalism to honor the memory of Katherine Graham by finding out what really happened to J. H. Hatfield, author of *Fortunate Son*, the Bush exposé conveniently squelched just before the election, who died of natural causes at 43? Silly me. Sap!

Just as the corn was getting high as a GOP elephant's eye, but before it was charred by whatever that was that fell from the sky—old Mir chunks? That long lost Mars Probe? Non-raptured evangelicals? Shards of the ABM treaty?—I began celebrating the imminent arrival of my tax rebate check by doing voluntary rolling blackouts with Jenna and Barbara. Whoopee!

The tax rebate is a lot like Bush [I can't hear you!] down in some rough and faux tumbleweed Texas watering hole, buying a round of drinks for everyone. They used to do it right on election day, but what with that unfortunate mess in sonny's Florida, it was unseemly.

It cost the IRS thirty million bucks to send out notices of that old punchline, "the check is in the mail." It's not just Dick who's fibbing better, because it turns out, the kickbacks are not for everyone.

The transparent vote buying made me so livid, I

improperly tore the three-sided perforated line on my notice when it arrived in the mail. I believe I made some chads. I loathe those who cavalierly say that $300 will buy them a moderately priced dinner in the Hamptons. Three hundred dollars is a huge needed cash influx for some people. As if they will ever see it.

We've started our own rebate renegade group, our motto is, "Payback is a bitch, so be one." We're pooling our money and going to choose one of the following group plans:

Pay Dick Cheney's utility bill. Old Tick is hooked up each night to his recharger and it costs. He wants the Navy, last I heard, one of those pesky government groups, to pay it for him. Hi, Sailor! Want to see my three-pronged adapter? We'll pay it, so the Navy doesn't have to do private fundraising luncheons on crowded submarines.

Underwrite a month of Weight Watchers in the White House. Started in May, the group chaired by Mr. Karen Hughes, meets every Tuesday, and has lost a total of 150 pounds. Help them lose 180 ugly pounds and impeach George Bush.

Hire our own private investigator to find out what did happen to J. H. Hatfield. We will not hire any investigators from the DC area. They are busy. They might get more done if they didn't spend so much time being interviewed by "fair and balanced" FAUX news.

Make little sachet bags for the Salvation Army Kettles come holiday time. I can't tell you everything that's in the goodie bag, suffice it to say that the aroma will be more fecal than faith based. And who knew a truck load of elephant dung could cost so much?

Sponsor as many new voting booths as we can afford for northern Florida. One of our members wanted to have little gold plaques with "This is James Baker Free Space" welded over each entrance, but she was voted down. Sponsorship of a "Keep Your Trifocals at Home" to prevent candidate/lever alignment errors, is being debated for Miami Dade County.

Invest in long-range, TelePrompTer scramblers for widespread civilian use. The small hand-held device emits a laser beam that shuts down W's TelePrompTers, effective within a three-block radius. Or invent them. Now.

(2001)

DOING A W-TAKE

ON A RECENT BUSINESS TRIP to Seattle, I was put up in the W Hotel. Fabulous! Whatever you like about your accommodations—the tasteful chenille throw on the fainting couch placed just so by the perfectly treated window, the 400-thread-count pillow shams, the reading light over the bed—you can order in their in-room catalogue. It was like an overnight in a high-end Pottery Barn. Everywhere are little tasteful, monogrammed Ws and each time I saw one, I did a W-take. They gave me the willies. That concerned me.

Apparently I've been driving people crazy, taking my job as Designated Bush Watcher a little too seriously. No one else seems to care. They don't want to hear it. I start talking about the latest Bush wacky idea and it's as if I've suddenly sprung a wicked case of middle school B. O. Put me in a cave and I could smoke 'em out.

So excuse me for harshing your mellow, for stepping on your smile. I for one am trying to learn to kick back and enjoy this war. And, come to find out that W in George's name doesn't just stand for War. There's a whole lot of wonderful W going on out there.

W—for women. There's that axis of estrogen around George—Matalin, Rice and Hughes. Tom Brokaw, in his day-in-the-life White House special, "Touched by a President," whispered reverentially, "They're right down the hall from him!" Bush is helping Liddy Dole to succeed Senator Jesse Helms in North Carolina, or as she stressed when announcing her candidacy, "I say succeed, for no one can replace him." FYI, Helms said he was sorry that he did not do more about AIDS. It was not clear what he meant.

W—for Winfrey. Heck, I'm not sweating politics any more. Forget that annoying political process. Bloomberg bought the New York mayoralty. Corzine bought himself a New Jersey Senate seat. I'd like to buy a vowel—O. Let's run Oprah for president with Martha Stewart as her running mate. Dr. Phil for Secretary of the Inferior.

W—for wealth. We can just hope that Enron and Arthur Anderson, where apparently every day was Casual Day, were not products of the math education program in Texas. They were just paying it forward. Thank goodness all that bankruptcy unpleasantness is just confined to Enron/Arthur Anderson. It is, right? Isn't it? With Clinton it was about him getting laid. With Bush it's about all of us getting Layed. Just as Phillip Morris, without hint of irony, has recently changed its name to Altria, from the Latin meaning "high," Enron should change its name to Blanca Casa.

W—for Winter Olympics. I for one was disappointed there was no Osmond tossing. Next time instead of medals, let's do pass/fail. I'm glad the Games are over, so I can settle down for the next stop on the Bread and Circus Circuit of diverting entertainment—aWard season. The Oscars, the Tonys, the ESPYs, The Golden People's Choice Awards, the Putting on Your Socks Best Awards.

W—for Wayback Machine. The Pentagon has a cool new Office of Information Awareness headed by John Poindexter. Despite his title he always declines to be interviewed. He specializes in data mining. For those of you who thought a Poindexter was a type of guy, not an actual guy, John was convicted in the Iran/Contra Reagan era scandal. That had to do with drug money for terrorists, not to be confused with the new ads from Bush's Drug program called Compassionate Coercion. It would be personally helpful for me and my delicate state if they would use that little Olympic upper left hand corner "Live" notation when some of these guys are speaking, if they ever speak.

W—for warming. Global that is. Here in the northeast it's been the warmest winter since records have been kept. And we're in drought condition. That old saying, "Everybody complains about the weather, but nobody does anything about it" is now wrong.

W—for Wahhabism—A dour reformed style of Islam, which stomped out the ornate, liberatory Sufi branch of Islam and made it possible for men to have relations with women, but only in the afterlife. I'm fascinated by those suicide bombers who believe they will be rewarded in paradise by 72 black-eyed virgins. Is it 72 per? Or 72 total? And how did they get those black eyes?

W—for Whoa! I'm veering again. Gonna take a chill pill, take a shower, go lie down, pop a couple of pretzels.

(2002)

JUGGERNAUT GEORGE

WHEN OLD JUGGERNAUT GEORGE READ to us that the increased border security would help the war on drugs, the anthrax scare would improve our healthcare system and increased surveillance would make people dress nicer in public, I saw my opportunity. Since then I have been following all the exciting new war technologies and am so looking forward to their peacetime, if there ever is such a thing again in my lifetime, use.

On many Internet search engines, there is a rich literature of breathless stories of the conversion of war technologies into peacetime doohickeys. Of course, we would not even have an Internet if it weren't for the MIT engineers hired by the Pentenron to improve their communication system, a.k.a. espionage. The wonders of Mapquest, a miracle for the directionally challenged like myself, are possible because of all the spy satellites beaming out global positioning system coordinates. I never get lost, but I often have the creepy feeling I'm being followed. Night vision goggles from George 43's Persian Gulf War are now widely used to hunt deer at night. And where would fashion be without the new beige camouflage?

Already we see some Operation Enduring Freedom, [new sanitary pad? military operation? you be the judge] technological advances creeping into daily use. Stealth bombs, whose major charm was that they destroy people and leave buildings standing, have yet to achieve their full utility among landlords and Scud missiles turned out to be as accurate as a Chuck Knoblach throw, but I see big promise with the new nuclear cave cleaners. Isn't it ironic that when we have weapons of mass destruction they're called nuclear, but when someone else has nuclear weapons they're weapons of mass destruction? Heck, put away your Mr. Clean, and cancel your cleaning lady, with just a thimbleful, spring cleaning is a thing of the past. Actually, if you use too much, spring is a thing of the past. And careful of those earthquakes!

Robot drones—it looks like Robert Dornan, but it's not—are the latest rage in unmanned aircraft. The robots do the dull and dangerous work that no one else wants to do. Like war. They are being quickly adapted for civilian use. Robo-accountants. Robo-security personnel. Someone should measure the level of human boredom in airports; it is dangerously toxic. Robot-droning TV personalities. Why do I feel like I'm drowning in a bucket of warm smarm whenever CNN's Aaron Brown assures me of something? Robo-Rome spokesmen condescendingly explain that we don't know what celibacy is. No, Clothman, you don't know what celibacy is.

The color scheme from Homeland "Security" Tom Ridge, the Roy G. Biv of terror, has lots of peacetime uses. Martha Stewart and Ralph Lauren are already spinning their color wheels, relieved to be released from all that red, white and blue. I'm concerned average citizens are without a proper mnemonic device to remember the pigment levels of alert under stress. It's Green, Blue, Yellow, Orange, Red or GBYOR. Try these: Gore's beard, yesterday's old ruse. George Bush, you're over reacting. Grim, bummer, yikes, oy, run!

Now I look at ordinary products and try to guess which military use it served. The new Listerine Oral Tabs are tiny but powerful strips of green which melt Listerine on your tongue. I was unaware that people were having such a hard time getting mouthwash to their mouths. The new delivery system comes in green packaging with a half life of about a billion years and should start washing up on beaches some-time this summer perfectly complimenting those pastel pink plastic tampon holders. I'm thinking the product was developed for HUMINT ground troops who needed to destroy information quickly and also needed to fend off the common cold in those Afghan winters. They feel fabulous trying to find Osama Bin Laden, and all the while, their breath smells minty fresh.

(2002)

WHOOPI CAUTION

BY PRESS TIME I WAS unable to obtain a copy of the tape of Whoopi Goldberg at the Madison Square Garden Concert for Kerry in which she donned black face with Ted Danson and did a schtick she wrote. No wait, that was 1993. At the Kerry fest, she carried a liquor bottle and did a twenty-minute riff on that double entendre gift bag of a word—"bush." Perhaps they were angry that is was too female. Better to be about his Dick Cheney. And his potty mouth.

The FOX of Warheads were characteristically outraged and demanded a tape of the event. There are double entendres and there are double standards, so I sent them my personal forty-three hour tape from the Clinton years with footage of their own hysterical jokes about Bill and his Willy. It was returned.

As if they weren't at the Kerry event. Somebody was there with a camera, because the next Sunday, people who had laughed or chuckled mildly during Whoopi's set were not allowed to receive communion in their churches. Bill Cosby dissed her just on principle. Lesbians wearing "Good Bush, Bad Bush" T-shirts were sent to Guantanamo. Janet Jackson sent Whoopi a thank you note.

While I was waiting for my taped evidence to arrive, Linda Ronstadt was booed off the stage at the Aladdin Theater in Las Vegas for dedicating an encore song, "Desperado" to Michael Moore. The chips fell where they may. Also drinks and coasters. She was "escorted" out of the hotel, tumbling onto the valet-swarming pavement with her luggage flying out the door after her.

The Aladdin management said that they had cancelled Ms. Ronstadt's engagement because she was there to entertain guests, not to impose her political views. Somebody needs a nap.

Speaking of shoving things down people's throats, after many customer complaints, the Slim Fast people "shed," "trimmed," or "dropped" Whoopi, as spokesperson for their product. Still no word if the cushion people will drop Whoopi, but who knew so many Republicans were on Slim-Fast? "I just want to lose ten pounds in case we have to cancel the elections." "That orange alert adds ten pounds." "Do these jack boots make me look fat?"

In solidarity with my sister comic, I tried to organize a protest to dump Slim Fast into the Provincetown Harbor. My permit was denied by the harbormaster who said the goo was too environmentally toxic. Especially the strawberry flavor. In their support of Whoopi, the Democrats announced that the humor of the Whoopster did not reflect the opinions of the Kerry campaign. That's when I found that there are rules about dumping Democrats into the harbor.

In addition to bailing on Whoopi, the Kerry "support" has had a chilling trickle-down effect on other groups. Unity 2004, a coalition of ten LGBT groups, disinvited comedian Margaret Cho from entertaining at their convention bash near the aptly named Fleet Center. The DNC denied any pressure, but the Human Rights Campaign said they pulled Cho after they previewed her material and found it "brutal" on Bush.

It seems that UPS is not the only group wearing brown shirts these days. From Tom Delay's chad thugs storming offices in Florida to the casino goondas to the values hoods on Fox, Bush can be a lightweight, because his heavies do his work. For the Democrat desperados, the beige of Kerry is the new brown. And the GLBT community can beat itself up just fine, thank you very much. Yellow is the new rainbow.

(2004)

THE FREEDOM TO MARY CHENEY

THE FRIDAY AFTER THE ELECTION, I was in a free-food-at-five courtesy suite at a hotel in Sacramento, eaves-dropping on a group of disgruntled straight professionals who were frothing about the unthinkable of the unthinker getting elected. I got up and stood by their table, and they went silent. Good to know I have not lost my high school teacher/cafeteria monitor mien.

"I'm sorry we were getting so loud," one woman said.

"Oh no," I answered. "I'd love to sit shiva with you."

I joined their Coalition of the Wailing, and as one woman quietly banged her forehead on the table, we davened for democracy. After stating a liberal tautology, one of the men concluded sadly, mystified, "But I guess I'm now in the minority on this." And I thought, "Well, how do you like it?"

But I did not say it because I didn't have the energy to come out as a lesbian and then explain to their perplexed faces how it was that 23 percent of the gay vote decided to win another girly mandate for that son of a Gipper.

For you, I'll explain. In the catastrophic success of the 2004 election, some gays said Bush's war on terror was more important to them than his war on gays. Some said that they felt radical gay activists had pushed the issue of gay marriage at the wrong time. Others denied that Bush had manipulated anti-gay marriage sentiment and blamed it on activist judges and radical gay activists. Some said gay issues were only 20 percent of what they based their vote on: More important were issues like a flat tax, school vouchers, or privatizing Social Security. Others said they did not vote for Kerry because he copped out on gay marriage, so they voted for Bush on other issues with which they agreed. To summarize: What's the matter with Kansas? Dorothy.

More to the point, unlike the straight vote, 77 percent of the gay vote went for the Democrats. They did not deserve it. Their public silence on the anti-gay rights initiatives in eleven states was shameful. If eleven states were attempting to pass initiatives limiting the civil rights of Jews or African Americans or Hispanics, there would have been an outcry. If the federal government had been seeking to amend the Constitution with the immoral value of bigotry, there would not have been such silence. But I guess I'm in the minority on that one.

In the vice presidential debate when John Edwards out-smarmed even Aaron Brown and said to the Vice Cusser, "Your daughter is a lesbian," it sounded like, "Bummer, man, too bad about your straight man's burden." When John "Bad Man" Kerry echoed that sentiment, he violated Don't Ask, Don't Tell and tipped all the undecided-on-their-values voters into the red of embarrassment.

Sometimes I try to walk a mile in Mary Cheney's sensible shoes. What was her Thanksgiving like? Dear old Dad side-mouthing the blessing, "Go fuck yourself," then carving up the turkey. "White or dark? And if you make the wrong choice, we could get hit again." And there really is no choice, because Dad and Antonin bagged the turkey with their unbanned assault rifles, so it's more of a turkey hash. SOS Condi was there with her famous mushroom cloud stuffing. Mary's "friend" was there, but seated at the kid's table. Lynne had positioned a lovely local straight lad next to Mary "just in case." On a scale of one to PFLAG, the Cheneys are a zero.

What the gay outsurgency got this election was not the Freedom to Marry, but the Freedom to Mary Cheney—to be cute and mute, and respected right back into the closet. In the Democrats' pathetic new quest to get religion metaphors, Mary Cheney is the Patron Saint of the Used. Cardinal Karl exploited her and the wedge issue of gay marriage to get out the fundamentalist vote.

That a thirty-five-year-old gay identity movement can so threaten a 2005-year-old Christian identity movement, though, is the good news.

(2005)

WEAPONS OF MASS DISTRACTION

．　　．　　．

The Y2K glitch came a little late this millennium. The buildup had been huge. Many twentieth-century—centric "best of" lists were made. Women and gays' numbers were unlisted. Techno-chaos was forecast, but would not even register orange on today's color code. Television's twenty-five hour dawn of the New Millennium coverage showed satellite's empiric reach like some global stadium wave. Bjork wore another weird outfit. But finally, in December 2000, the glitchiest glitch of all occurred when W won the presidency by a vote of 5 to 4. That was the first wave of shock and awe. September 11, 2001 was the second. The third was the war on terror, subsequently repackaged as "Freedom is on the march." Freedom does not march. It saunters, meets up with friends, goes to a movie, has sex in the afternoon, maybe goes dancing, then has a dreamy night's sleep under cool, clean sheets.

Playing Telephone

ON ELECTION DAY I HAD a major computer meltdown. I won't mention any names or brands. Macintosh Power-Book 5300cs. I don't want to get too technical on you, but the cs stands for crock o' shit. I called my local repair person and described to her what was not happening, i.e., the laptop was not speaking to the printer. She said, "Sounds like you've blown your logic card."

She continued, "It's a design problem on that model. Bring it down to the shop, and we'll take a look under the hood."

TekServe is a great place. It's total grunge. The repair people could as easily be fixing bikes as computers. The door chime is the sound of a Mac booting up. A red antique soda machine sells ten-cent pony bottles of Coke. In one corner is an old computer terminal screen, its guts replaced by a very active ant farm.

My squeeze helped me lug the printer and cables and laptop in a taxi down to the repair shop. She was rushing off to work. We got stuck in traffic. Neither of us had time for this MacInconvenience. I looked over at her and said, "We've got to relax." She spontaneously redigitalized what I said to her, looked puzzled, then slightly annoyed, and responded, "We've got three legs?"

This mishearing is going around. Maybe Californians had a hard time understanding the wording of Proposition 209. Maybe they were confused that no meant yes, yes meant no. Maybe they were hopelessly muddled about whether one positive plus one negative plus one positive—"I am in favor [+] of eliminating [-] affirmative [+] action"—equals a negative. Or a positive. I am trying to give them the benefit of the doubt. Oh heck, I was headlining at the Benefit of the Doubt. Then I heard how Texaco was trying to cover its oily ass. The company basically claimed that its executives were playing that old party game called "Telephone," just repeating what they thought they had heard. That's what the redigitalized tapes were about. Soon they were back at their old game—Monopoly. Only they were losing: Go directly to settlement, do not pass go.

Good for the plaintiffs, bad for those of us anxious to hear more redigitalized hooey. Instead of "Black jelly beans stick to the bottom," how about, "Jack's really been sick this autumn?" Instead of, "I'm still having trouble with Hanukkah. Now we have Kwanzaa?" perhaps, "I'm still having trouble with my Honda. Now a Nissan Stanza?" You know I can't hear you when the oil's running.

It's going around. Turns out David Brinkley, on ABC's

innovative election-night version of *Candid Camera,* had not described President Clinton as "nothing but a bore spouting goddamned nonsense for four more years." A couple of nights later an unchagrined Mr. Wrinkley apologized to a stern Mr. Clinton. He said it was a late night, he was dead tired, and he thought he was giving a critical theater review, "Nothing like *HMS Pinafore,* that goddamned *Nunsense* runs for four more years." Apology accepted; hugs withheld.

The most brazen use of digitalized disclaimers comes from people who voted to reelect President Clinton. After watching the Clintonistas doing a victory dance that involved jumping ship, another flip-flop on a balanced-budget amendment, and Bill and Hill whining Down Under, many voters were heard muttering "I doted for kittens," "I voted for quittin'," and "I voted for Klingons."

(1997)

Connecting the Sects

ON CUE EVERY YEAR, THOUSANDS of lesbians of all ages flock to Palm Springs for the Dinah Shore Golf Classic. As the green oasis sucks the nearby aquifers dry, the women celebrate amidst hundreds of thousands of chat-chomping college students in jeeps and humvees, armed for spring break with high-powered water rifles.

It could be a lethal clash of cultures. But the two sects hardly intersect, since the lesbians shut themselves inside huge, hermetically sealed hotels, gated and designated for fun and sun worship—all by the grace of Tanqueray. As the spring sun drifts toward the west, they turn their lounge chairs and prayer towels in sun-dialed, choreographed ritual.

The annual lesbian purification by chlorine and Coors commemorates the goddess Dinah Shore, patron saint of

GMC. She was the first woman to break the tinted glass ceiling of car sales when her dulcet voice lured people into buying Chevrolets to see the USA. Even though she left her vehicle a couple of earth years back, the rite continues.

Since the Rancho Santa Fe mass suicides, everything seems like a cult. The Dinosaur Desert Classic, the Tennessee Lady Vols, Pat Summit and her blue eye shadow and Rajneeshy orange, AA, the Twelve Apostles, AOL.

Californians aren't taking it well. The newspapers are filled with whining why-me's: "Jim Jones and O.J. and Lyle and Eric and the riots and Bob Dornan—and now this?!" And psycho ceramics are all the rage. These crackpot theories claim, "It's the weather, it's the water, it's Jerry Brown." One guy, head of Way Out Productions, a missing-persons search firm, record label, long-distance phone company, and talent agency, said, "It's the flavor of the day, the X-files waiting to happen." He's already pitching America's Weirdest Home Videos.

Dan Rather, at least, was in heaven. He made more connections than an NRA lobbyist at the Republican convention. He tried so hard because he had to play catch-up, since his network was not the first to throw its MASS SUICIDE logo and creepy music up on the satellite feed.

As if connecting all those dots would make a picture, Dan drew lines between Jim Jones and alienation and Gnosticism and Easter and resurrection and ancient times and yellow marshmallow peeps and Bo and Peep and cloning and losing sheep and not knowing where to find them and then finding them wearing Nikes and the JUST DO IT mantra and the swoosh icon like some big checkoff on the road to the final four and computers and comets and Hale Boggs and Charles Manson and his parole denied which was fine with Chuck because he wanted to keep working on his web site, www.swastika.forehead, and the big web page in the sky and Dan went on and on until I began to think those poor Higher Source people were on to something and the least they could have done is taken Dan with them.

The subplot I always dreaded broke soon enough. The leader of the cult had lost his college teaching position allegedly because he had sex with a young male student. The college denied it had let him go for moral reasons. But he did submit to a program for sexual reorientation. No one in the press pointed out that the program was a dismal failure.

Speaking of sects, Jerry Falwell's church has urged Johnson & Johnson, Chrysler, and GMC to pull their advertising from *Ellen*. Falwell called her "Ellen Degenerate" as if there were a second grader left who hadn't come up with that one already. And in more sectual news, the Presbyterian Church, after years of rancorous debate, voted to require all unmarried ministers, deacons, and elders to be sexually celibate. The Chastity [not Bono] Amendment is a cowardly back-door attempt to avoid outright banning of the ordination of homosexuals. Presbyterian conservatives are thrilled. Stop me before I connect again, but can a Sacrament of Castration be far behind?

(1997)

LISTOMANIA

ALL YEAR, LISTS AND PARODIES of lists have been appearing regularly in newspapers, magazines and books throughout the country. There have been so many "best of" shows on television, it must soon inevitably spawn the List Channel. In the last few months of the millennium it's bound to get worse.

There are two general types of lists—action or information. We all have action lists. I have lists of lists—things to do, people to call, things to pick up at A&P. Of course sometimes, this organizing principle can list into the realm of obsession and Post-its flutter around me like queens around Cher. Thank goodness for the glass-encased "to do" list of my Palm Pilot.

We're all crazy busy people and we need to get our info fast. We're curious. So if someone—anyone—presorts for us, we are only too happy to be list-served. Whether it's Internet info overload, acute David Lettermania, some final millennial spasm of cataloguing of all of the above, we are undeniably in taxonomic shock.

Curiously, despite our thousandth-year anniversary, it is an oddly twentieth-century–centric moment. There are no "Neat Folks of the Millennium" lists—the Queen of Sheba [1000], Joan of Arc and Shakespeare [1400], Suleiman the Magnificent [1500], Catherine the Great [1700]. We can't seem to handle anything but the twentieth century foxes.

VH1 just aired "The 100 Greatest Women of Rock and Roll." PBS broadcast the best in photojournalism, which was great if you can't get enough of war. Award shows are nothing more than prioritized lists with prizes. Awesomest Babe of the Universe. The People's Choicest Awards. MTV has their cheeky Movie Awards. [Sidebar: let me be the first to nominate MTV for their coverage of Woodstock II in the category of Best Straight White Race Riot.]

Coffee-table books like *The Century* [the American is understood] are selling fast, especially if they are long on photos. Fortunately, Tom Brokaw and Peter Jennings have taken time out of their busy schedules as anchor hawkers and self-appointed grief counselors, to explain everything to us in their books that Stephen Spielberg hasn't gotten around to yet.

The New York Times Magazine, in their listing tour, has busily catalogued the most powerful thinkers, inventors, celebrities of the century. The ratio of people of color in the top 100 is so mathematically minuscule, it feels more ration then ratio. If these lists were discovered in a time capsule centuries from now, historian could only conclude that Bill Cosby and Jesse Jackson were very busy men. And there are hardly any black women because apparently they are all too busy taking care of the children of the New York-based magazine editors who are busy making lists of those who matter.

The *Times* seems to be listing to the right these days. Their separatist issue "Women, the Shadow Story of the Century" entitled them not to talk about women again until 3000. I found the article online, typed in the word "lesbian," and hit the Find button on my toolbar. It was highlighted three times and the coded "same-sex" was used twice. Five glancing references to lesbians in the century, but who's counting? I am.

Of course, retrospectives are by definition retro. Whenever I pore over these century lists, I feel as if I am paging through the yearbook of some giant Straight High School: 2 straight 2 be 4 gotten. I feel like I used to feel watching for gay clues in early Lily Tomlin specials, looking forward to the bimonthly gay question in Sunday's Parade Magazine, or waiting for someone to choose Paul Lynde to block. It's very retro, this looking for representations of myself and my friends, made more desperate, incredulous, hopeful, furious by the great closet-smashing work of the Gay '90s of this century.

It has been the Straight White Century. True, lists are not history. But next time around, I say, "No taxonomy without representation."

(1999)

Gaydar Love

A Canadian entrepreneur—two words you just don't hear enough in tandem—recently patented a small pocket device that can be carried by gay men to detect the presence of other gay men. Instead of a well-placed hand-kerchief, pinky ring, or rainbow decal, the little wonder picks up signals the guys are giving off. The device can also be set to "female" for lesbo-detection. Gender equity has long been a hallmark of the Canadian psyche.

When the gizmo is activated by an electronic impulse from another, a beep sounds or a light blinks. One hopes that in the future design requirements, a vibrating function will be added, not only for the pleasure principle, but also for noise abatement amidst the already deafening racket of the Cellutlites.

"Hey, is that a cell phone in your pocket, or are you just glad to see me?"

Demonstrating that he has learned from H. Ty Warner, the marketing genius behind the Beanie Baby craze, the Canadian entrepreneur will not ship his invention until 40,000 units are sold over the Net in selected markets. He claims this is so a gay man will not be further traumatized to discover that, given his new device, he is still the only gay person in the room.

The developer has been stymied thus far, not by any technical difficulties but by trademark problems. The rights to the name "Gaydar" are in dispute in this domain-crazed world. So let me offer some optional names for the homo-homing box: Yamagaychi, Beanie Gaybies, Tickle Me Homo, or Dirty Chatty Kathy.

Of course, I'm old fashioned enough to worry that this gadget will fall into the wrong hands and that more violence will be done to gay men and lesbians. Please don't give one to Jesse "The Boil" Helms.

I've always felt like I was born into the wrong century. With new developments like this in the past few months, I've been feeling twice as lost. But now I'm trying to change my mainframe; I'm seeing this as an opportunity to be as out of it as I thought my parents were.

I do. I have no choice. I never would have thought that a widget would replace a wink, that a huge online business would be called Amazon.com, that Larry King would find the groove thing of David Crosby's sperm, or that ABC's *Who Wants to Be a Millionaire?* would do more to normalize gays in America than anything else in the last few years. Regis Philbin is our Rosa Parks?

The sun never sets on the AOL/Time Warner empire. ABC's twenty-five-hour coverage of the dawn of the new millennium presaged he empire's reach like some global stadium wave. Since the merger announcement, I've had nothing but problems. So many people in my Time Warner quadrant tuned into the premiere of *The Sopranos,* that lovable, dysfunctional Mafia family (as opposed to other unlovable, but fully functional Mafia families), that the cable system went down like the drop in water pressure during Super Bowl halftime.

Near-fatal errors have occurred in my e-mail. Someone posing as me broke up with a friend of mine, who remains oddly hurt despite my gentle reminders that we never dated.

To remedy the problem, I had to contact the "AOL Community Action Team." I have not gotten through yet. In fact, I wrote this entire article while on hold. I now know what "the thrill of hope" is that makes the weary world rejoice. It's when you are on hold, listening to the banal whine of Kenny G., and the music suddenly stops. The thrill is in that nanosecond of quiet when you sense you will finally talk to an actual person—before the hope is dashed by another voice that begins, "Thank you for calling AOL. All of our representatives are currently helping other customers."

(2000)

REALLY SIX FEET UNDER

THE REALITY OF TELEVISION FOR me is that I haven't been able to watch much since the Bush Cryo-Junta. Even the solace of the Weather Channel is gone because Florida still dangles there as a limp reminder. When Walker, Texas Ranger was canceled, I was shocked to learn it had been on for nine seasons. It had always looked like a rerun, perhaps because Chuck Norris's hair had remained the same despite incredible advances in the follicular sciences.

Ever since the Nutworks and the Supreme Court ordered up four years of The W-Files, it too has had the humid air of a summer rerun. Old ideas-evil empires, abortion, oil oligarchies, Star Wars, Clinton reimpeachment, gay invisibility. Old guys—Tick Cheney, Ariel Sharon, Donald

Rumsfeld. It's like Antiques Roadshow, but without any gay men telling us how much our stuff is worth.

When W. was not "thinking hard about stem cell research" on his "working vacation" at home in the heartland, where he had once awaited his foregone selection, his aides previewed the syndicate's Fall Values. Their goal is to show the real Bush—not some airborne tumbleweed bouncing by, rootless, able to survive in an arid land—but the Bush who is "thoughtful" and "ruminative." Deep.

They're looking for spectators, not citizens. Bush is so TV. He is That '70s Show. Everything new is old again. The "new" season is bringing us more reality shows, more white guys talking to each other, more blonds, more humiliation, more openly closeted people, more fair and balanced unfair unbalanced propaganda.

CNN promises, "We're doing things different." Like what? Not using adverbs? Not using chairs? So many CNN-chor people are standing, it looks like open mike night at Caroline's Comedy. They do stagy head turns to interview talking heads on Jambi screens with market quotes, headlines, weather, all blinking like an optic migraine I once had. Obviously they have laid off all their gay designers. They are trying to bring in the younger viewer or touch off adult-onset ADD. Has the Ritalin patent run out yet?

When we pick up that thick, glossy TV Guide Fall Preview, here are a few shows we may be seeing.

Everybody Loves Ronald
Though he tripled the deficit and never mentioned the word "AIDS," Ronald Reagan was our go-to guy. Now

watch Bush 43 turn into a chip off the old Gip, especially at nap time!

McCain in the Middle

The pilot shows the hilarious demonization of this nutty little Republican. He'd rather be a prisoner of war for eight years than have a private meeting with Cheney in Tick's private office, known affectionately as "The Torture Chamber." Ha-ha!

My Four Sons

Dick "Hey, Collagen Man!" Clark says he wants to produce a show like *The View* for men, because "women don't get to see four men sitting around talking." I ran my irony meter over the statement, and the needle did not move. Let's start with Barb's boys, the un-Kennedys, sharing about baseball stadiums, offshore drilling, and being born again again.

Whose Line Is It Anyway?

Not the improv show that is the only thing I can safely watch these days. It's interactive! You'll parse a speech from Bush's brilliant speechwriters. Hit your buzzer when you hear tautology: "It is American because it is America"; metaphor: "Rocks in the storm, feathers in the wind"; or exaggeration: "When the American people elected me."

Who Wants to Be a Petromillionaire?

You can get all the family lifelines and audience help you want. Instead of ominous music, we'll do rolling blackouts. It's not for everyone!

Faux Headline News

Rupert Murdoch's guys and blonds fume over crises like
Bill Clinton's $10 million book deal. He got more than the
Pope! It's obscene!

(2001)

Chick Chick Hooray!

JUST SO YOU KNOW, THE Dixie Chicks make me proud to be a lesbian. They are an Axis of Excellent Straight Women. Fending off a hard-charging, devil's-advocating, Diane Sawyer on a recent Primetime Live, the Chicks stood their ground, and lo, Sawyer was reduced to a Mighty Wind. But more of that later.

Sawyer, the former Nixon speechwriter with the ice-blue gaze, might have fared more mightily interviewing someone with less on the ball. Like, say, Sen. Rick "The P Is Silent" Santorum, when he listed the right to consensual sex within your own home with the other alienating rights to bigamy, polygamy, incest, adultery, and the very intriguing "right to anything."

His remarks in that Associated Press interview have been defended and decried, contextualized and criticized. A polygamist from a breakaway Mormon sect demanded a retraction. Pennsylvania's other senator, Arlen Sphincter, defended his junior partner. And according to spokesmeister Ari Fleischer, our Commando-in-Chief feels that Sen. Sanscrotum is "inclusive." That's the Shock-enaw tribe's word for "little flap on big tent."

The fact of the matter is, that giant sucking sound you heard was Sanatorium trying to make up to conservatives who were furious at him. He had watered down a provision of the Bush faith-based initiative that would have helped religious groups get government grants. That had won him the praise of the Human Rights Campaign—another reason he had to distance himself by throwing out some gay bait.

But people, not enough has been made of the poor interviewer. In the unedited Associated Press text, not only do you get to see the full shallowness of Sanctimoron's logic, but you also get to see the dangers of sending a squeamish, apologetic reporter to do a Sawyer-size job.

After trying to get a clarification of "the right to privacy lifestyle" and wading into the ethical quagmire of homo-sexual being vs. doing, the interviewer asked Sen. Sancti-monious if he would argue "without being too gory or graphic" that homosexuals should not have sex. Incoming! This led the junior senator to an earnest disquisition on marriage and, ultimately, to "man on dog" sex. French poodles have demanded an apology.

While the third-ranking senator oozed sadly that the state does not have rights "to limit individuals' wants and passions" [the yet was understood], the interviewer strug-gled to recover: "I'm sorry, I didn't think I was going to talk about 'man on dog' with a U.S. senator, it's sort of freaking me out."

According to Bill Bennett, odds are that Sawyer would have had a follow-up question, but don't bet the ranch. Whether it's rolling around on the floor in Little Havana with Elian Gonzalez, or squinting down Florida Rep. Randy Ball about gay adoption, Sawyer is deeply embedded in Aaron Brown-strength smarm.

Which brings us back to the Dixie Chicks' historic Primetime win. I admit I did not hear the entire interview, because for a good part of it, my galpal was screaming about Mrs. Mike Nichols on the ABC Primetime comment line. But my highly intuitive Tivo caught it all for my prepro-grammed "Gay Pride Highlights" reel.

If you are planning to come out to some family or friend this month, study the Sawyer Inquisition footage for pointers. For what to do when attempts are made to shame you, watch the irrepressible Natalie Maines respond that speaking out is a most patriotic thing do. She is steely, complex, engaging. When Diane presses her to ask for for-giveness, Maines counters by asking for acceptance of an apology already made. She does not ask for forgiveness of who she is. Diane plays a stunned condescension that says, "Gollee, you're pretty smart for Dixie hicks." When she tries to get the other Chicks to girl-gang up on Maines, they are not having any of it, and proudly amplify their friend's remarks. There's no rule that says you can't bring a friend to accompany you on a coming-out adventure.

If you need a refresher on how to be a proud fierce lesbian —and in these days of hypermacho in the flyboy zone who wouldn't?—stick with the Chicks, unrepentant, questioning, wild, patriotic, smart, loyal, honest, successful. Thank god they're our country girls.

(2003)

Weapons of
Mass Distraction

GOT TO HURRY UP AND finish this column—Ari Fleischer is leaving his job to spend more time with his new wife who was last seen running screaming from the house. I want that job.

After weeks of breathless headlines, jut-jawed military guys poking maps and talking game plans, and Commando in Chief flyboy nailing his landing to give us some closure don'tchaknow, I wondered what the first nonwar news item to merit this "coverage" would be. We all knew it would not be that messy freedom and cleanup. We've got to move on! Sing it: Freedom's just another word for nothin' left to loot!!

Bill Bennett bet he knew what it would be and wanted me to place a wager, but I demurred. [Bennett's bet: Annika Sorenstam desecrating the Colonial, came in fourth.]

Before the BBC revealed that the Pvt. Jessica Lynch tale had been wagged, before Laci Peterson's husband was charged with double murder of the born and unborn, the story that merited Faux News treatment was the now infamous Powder Puff football game in Illinois.

The game, a twenty-year tradition of sport and underage drinking at Glenbrook North High School, featuring hazing instead of cheerleading, got out of hand this year. It might have gotten out of hand other years too, but this time an unembedded amateur videographer fed CNN some raw footage of senior girls dumping mud, garbage and feces on junior girls. Whatever happened to after-prom bowling and hurling in the limo?

The pooper scoop was picked up, of course, by FOX who can sniff out a story. They took it and ran with it. Bill O'Really was shocked. It was awful. The grainy footage was run over and over.

Dirty girl-on-girl action, something Clarence Thomas might like in a video. Lord of the Fly Girls. They slowed it down, zoomed in on the cowering juniors in numbered jerseys looking like teenaged Prisoners of Whatever. I thought one of the hazing seniors looked like a young Ann Coulter but I could not be sure.

Get out those lazy, crazy, hazing days of summer! The Girls' Bully Bowl was a weapon of mere distraction from the Bush Putsch to tax cuts.

In a strategy called, "Flood the Zone" designed by Coach Karl Rove, eighty separate events in three weeks were designed to sling mud, dump garbage and buckets of crap. As if he were reading to us kids again, George said we don't need itty bitty tax cuts, we need some Daddy Bear-sized tax cuts.

The Powder Puff Girl's story also distracted from the Donald who told the Senate that he needed some itty bitty nuclear weapons to bust bunkers filled with evil-doers. Pentagoners call them mini-nukes and make them sound like baby carrots or tiny corns at the salad bar. At this point, the Hazer in Chief wants to develop the nuke lites, not to use them. Like Lenny just wanting to pet the rabbits. And I mean no insult to Lenny.

When asked recently if he felt that increased security measures were a threat to civil liberties, John Ashcroft said that he thought both could co-exist. To illustrate, he warmed as best he could, to a story. When he goes to his ranch in Missouri, he likes to head out to this barn and work on his hobby—no, not draping tiny blue burkas on Justice Barbies—making wire sculptures. He proudly announced that he had recently fashioned a statue of Lady Liberty entirely out of barbed wire. Color me secure. That he did it is one thing. That he told it as heartwarming illustration of the union of security and civil rights is a chilling other.

Watch for an ice carving of Justice Blindfolded by Antonin Scalia. W's head in papier mâché elephant dung bust for Mt. Rushmore by Karl Rove. A spent uranium fuel rod miniature of the Washington Monument by crank yanker Rumsfeld.

Talk about piling on.

(2003)

MEN BEHAVING
BADLY

・   ・   ・

Mae West once opined, "Most men want to protect me. Can't figure out from what." We are trapped in some ancient father-son drama. A quagmire. How far back did Cher turn time? To pre-feminist, pre-magnon, pre-emptive days? "Go to therapy. Quit taking it out on us." It is a manly man time. They are whacked out on Viagra and have a false sense of their own potency. Iraq is crack and they are on it. "Who's your Daddy?" is a tortured question. In the archetypal story, God the father, says to his son, "You are my son, in whom I am well pleased," and then the son dies a horrible death, captured on film years later by Mel Gibson. In Aramaic. But after they let all the gay translators go. The point is: the reward system for good behavior among men is not what it's cracked up to be.

The Big Dirt Nap Lottery

BEFORE JIM JEFFORDS JUMPED SHIP, our sister progressive magazine, The Nation, recently had a great cover caricature of the orange-hued, chia-haired Strom Thurmond with an accompanying article "Strom Watch" about the makeup of the Senate on his demise. The article began with a few tortured, apologetic sentences on the unseemliness of the death watch. I ran the article through my home metal detector for any traces of irony and the needle barely shivered.

No mention of the unseemliness of the death of democracy or of the now necessary reliance on the Grim Reaper with his big Term Limits in the Sky instead of that old nutty "voting" to affect the makeup of the Senate. Keep an eye for an eye out for the continued, counter-balancing, character assassination of Senator Robert Torricelli.

But alas, Jim Jeffords beat the clock.

With this administration, which I have begun to think of more as murder-suicide pact, all bets are off on the seemliness scale. The sheer vulgarity of its intergalactic arrogance, under the guise of dress codes, trains running on time and father knows bestness has raised an equal and opposite reckless incivility in me. It's my new faith and the fundament of my, fingers crossed, soon to be federally funded Church.

However, until we get those funds, and believe me, the paperwork is a killer, I've got a great idea for a fundraiser. No mere Uno Homo Morto speculation for us! It's The Big Dirt Nap Lottery!! Send a tax-deductible check made out to, "The Kate Clinton Enough Already with the Bispartisanshit Church" for ten dollars, more, if you really want us to pay attention, and put the following in order of their deaths: Dick Cheney, The Pope, Strom Thurmond, Jesse Helms, and now, for extra credit Timothy McVeigh.

Your contribution is tax deductible. If enough people participate, the returns will be grand and by the time we know the results, you are going to need the money, despite that big inverted Pyramid Scam, I mean, tax cut. I got a $2.16 rebate! They really are the party of change.

And because, message: we care, here are some tips, in no particular order, to help you in your particular order.

The Pope.

Although he recently starred in Greece, but who hasn't at this point, [and we can't wait to see him in *The Vagina Monologues*] and apologized for the Fourth Crusade, no word yet on the First through Third or Fifth through the current continuing antigay crusade. That fourth Crusade was eight hundred years ago and although I am sleeping better because of that apology, the College of Cardinals just met in Rome and though they deny it, that's like having Dr. Kevorkian pay you a hospital visit.

Dick Cheney.

Wouldn't you love to have his health care? He's amazing! What energy crisis? Only thing he's missing is the pink bunny suit and the little tin drum. He's the Czar of Everything, which makes me suspect he was cloned during some hospitalization. Or the Disney Animatronics people paid a late night visit. Get out your push pins, it's going to be a tough call.

Strom Thurmond.

Willard Scott is chomping at the bit. That orange dye is laced with some Ponce de Leon anti-aging formula. Turns out he's a big deterrence for more women in the Senate. If the grand prize at the end of your senatorial campaign, election and swearing-in is a big hug and slobbering kiss from that old state's rights coot, you might reconsider and just run for the real power position, head of your local elections commission.

Jesse Helms.

All bets are off. He's got a new rig and maybe a new understanding of disability access in the Senate, but his batteries are way charged. He even went to Mexico. Oil of Ole! My grandma often said that there are some people just too mean to die.

Timothy McVeigh.

Oops. So Hillary Clinton isn't the only one who misplaces

files. And, mind you, it's just the FBI and just this once that evidence has turned up missing. John Ashcroft, who himself lost a senate seat to a dead man but won the Department of Justice, might have painted himself into a the death penalty box with his stay statements. But probably not. My home irony meter went off scale on this one. Timothy McVeigh, willing to die for what he perceives are FBI Waco errors, lives to die another day because of FBI "errors" in his case.

God forbid Yogi Berra dies. The man who as a boy dreamed of one day becoming Commissioner of Baseball, our Sport Utility President, seems to be using the presidency as a stepping stone to that field of dreams, will be devastated. The Comish made an executive order to bring the people's sport to the White House backyard. But we know he cares more about T-bills than T-ball.

(2001)

Being John Ashcroft

During the presidential campaign, W's nannies had him meet with The Log Cabin Syrup Republicans. After, and after a shower no doubt, he said in typical Bush Vaguespeak, that he had learned a few things. It's true he hasn't worn any of those turquoise western wear bolos. In public. But he seems to have had front row seats at the movie "Being John Ashcroft" and liked what he saw. He wasn't the only one.

The Ashcroft-kissing Congress listened to the former senator's lies under oath about not obstructing Jim Hormel's ambassadorship based on his sexual orientation as if they were the truth, and, sans filibuster, confirmed him. You can see it in the new movie remake, Mr. Integrity asked to be sworn in by Clarence Uncle Thomas under cover of night. May Christopher Dodd be plagued by boils on his Connecticut yanker.

Perhaps because this is a Viagra-powered coup or because these guys are taking hits off Andrew Sullivan's testosterone drip, it is a very manly man time. Include Karen Hughes. It is thus a very de-gayed moment. After the unpleasantness in Florida, even the very circuit-party-boy-sounding "Chad" has been scared straight.

Despite the hushed reverential reminders that the Cheneys have a gay daughter, whenever the suckups we call the press hush hush whispered, "Look there she is at the swearing in and she's with her partner," the word "partner" sounded less domestic and more western and you half-expected to see tumbleweed bounce by. There might be something about Mary, but she can't signify for all. And let's review: only Dick Cheney, The Bush Whisperer, has the gay daughter. His lovely wife, Lon Cheney, demurs on the dyke thing.

Heck, even before Bill Clinton was elected, during the Clinton I vs. Bush I campaign, there was that wonderful photo of Bill and Al's head airbrushed onto two inter-twined buffed and barechested guys in denim cutoffs. The fun couple appeared on T-shirts, cards, and ads. I bet Bill and Al even had a laugh about it. It won't happen with Dick and W. Double phew. And if it did, the owners of Don't Panic would be executed in Texas as soon as they could be fit into the rotation.

Not two minutes into his administration, Bill Clinton was already deep in gays in the military doo-doo. Sam Nunn, Little Miss Fistula, had already taken his colleagues on a submarine field trip to show them just how close the quarters were. Don't ask. And how unsafe it was to pick up a bar of soap in the shower. They were in there for hours.

Don't tell. But whether the talk was for or against gays in the military, at least there was talk about gays somewhere.

About two minutes into the Bush Restoration and despite Showtime's ten million dollar ad campaign for and about the A-gays of *Queer as Folk,* it's like we're living in an Ex-gay ad sponsored by some faith-based group. Until now I have not supported outing because it is antichoice and punitive, but after Ricky Martin performed at the Inauguration and was photographed mugging with J. Fred W, I have changed my mind. Now, I like to wander into Tower Records and stand in front of the display of Ricky's new cry for help CD titled "Sound Loaded," and say to prospective teen girl buyers, "Did you know he's a big fag?"

We might never know exactly what George W. said to Al on the phone, when Al told him that he was not going to concede the presidential election after all. Whatever the major league hissy fit, Al said, "Well, there's no need to get snippy about it."

Days later, after he'd been to his ranch near Waco—after he'd had the boil lanced, the teleprompters installed in his retinas, and the blink sequencer regulated—W was asked in a ranch style press conference what he had said that had caused Al to characterize his behavior as snippy.

In his beige Stetson, watched over by a gloating Trent Lott also in a Stetson but looking like the guy from Toy Story, W said snippily, "Snippy? That's not a word we use in Texas. That's some northeast, smarty-pants faggoty word." He did not add. He didn't have to.

(2001)

Lay Off Bush

IT IS NOT PRETTY WHEN straight white guys experience the powerlessness of terror for the first time. They panic. They lash out. They speak rashly. They hide the gals. They get all manly man. Nobody can tell them anything. They don't want to hear it.

With the threat/promise of a ground war, the Bush Putsch has conveniently revoked Clinton's failed "Don't Ask, Don't Tell" policy in the military. Not to worry, they have invoked it everywhere else.

When the unspeakably arrogant "spokesman" Ari Fleischer warned, "Americans had better watch what they say," my sang froided. Is it cold in here or is it me? The mantra of Roy Cohn's lovechild is generally an aggrieved, peeved, "How dare you ask that?"

Tom Ridge is now head of something that sounds like those hexagonal blue signs people poke in their lawns. "This house is protected by Homeland Security" and we all know it's not hooked up to anything. In his very briefings, he bug-eyes, "Don't know, can't tell."

Attorney General J. Edgar Ashcroft, emphasis on the general, got his 500-page USA Patriot Antiterrorism Bill passed with little objection. The sound you hear is the shredders chewing up the Fourth Amendment. No one even knows where the Surgeon General is. Don't care, go to hell.

And everywhere, any dissent is drowned out with hooligan chants of USA! USA! USA!—the new, politically correct way to say Shut up! Shut up! Shut up!

To paraphrase some queen, it has been an annus horribilis. Since the red/blue polarizing presidential selection crisis of last November, I had already found, both personally and professionally, that it was easier to come out as lesbian than as a justice-loving progressive.

I first noticed this unsettling shift last December, when I did a show in Palm Beach, Florida—ground zero during the election crisis. The theater audience, a loyal subscription-series crowd intermixed with my Florida gay following, was breath-held-in-whole nervous during my political material. I could hear all of them exhale "Phew!" when I talked about being a lesbian.

During my summer shows in Provincetown, since no one was watching television, except for *West Wing*, I refined my public service job as the Designated Bush Watcher. Someone had to do it. The only cheer I could spin was that perhaps this was the last blast of the blasted straight white guys. I worried aloud that the problem was they might take us down with them.

Often I would see people get up and leave during Bush Bash section of the show. I pretended they had small bladders or needed to go out for a smoke.

In September I had a light performance schedule and any shows I had in the weeks following September 11 were mercifully canceled. I couldn't have gotten to them anyway. Including the one down on Broadway and 50th.

National Coming Out Day, October 11, was one of my first outings. I performed at a benefit in Boston for Speakout, a speaker's bureau which for thirty years has been sending gay men and lesbians to schools, community groups, and churches to tell their stories about being gay Americans and to answer questions. They were gay toastmasters, long before people got toaster ovens for coming out.

Like all marginal groups that last more than six months, Speakout has changed tactics with the times and currently they are tailing hired signature-shaggers trying to put a measure on the state ballot to make gay marriage illegal and impossible forever in the Bay State. One Speakout volunteer told me how at an area mall she had shadowed a young guy with a clipboard, who told her he'd been kicked out of his house in Arizona, that he was virtually homeless, probably bisexual and tired of selling his body. For him it was a job. Her goal was to keep him talking so he wouldn't get signatures. She said they are not all that easy.

On that month's anniversary of September 11, I was shell-shocked as we all were, emotionally speedballing between a freaky fatalistic serenity and blind murderous panic about nuclear war. When I wasn't feeling, well, silly, about things gay. The courageous asking and telling of Speakout's gay ground troops completely re-inspired me.

Audiences are traumatized. They are happy to be out, i.e., of the house. They laugh hysterically, glad for any release. It's easy to go easy. I could just do jokes, "Celine Dionne goes into a bar, bartender says, 'Why the long face?'" The current comedy coda is to lay off Bush. Stand behind the president. Only if I can put fingers behind his head. I fight self-censorship. I am trying to see this as an opportunity for change. Help me out here. Ask. Tell. Scream. Yell.

(2001)

THE CHARM OFFENSIVE

IT'S NOT THAT MY POST Election Traumatic Stress has totally disappeared. The sleep disorder continues. I have nightmares I've been dropped into a Bush family therapy session—the father/son thing, the revenge cycle, the brother's sibling rivalry, the mother-in-law, the twin daughters with their website twinsistersstuff.com. Check it out, you can get a T-shirt with the Bushfilles' faces on it!

My Bushtourrettes Syndrome continues. While Bush gave himself goosebumps reading his rocks in the stream, feather in the wind, angels in the whirlwind inaugural speech, I was like that little braided hair von Trapp Family girl after Julie Andrews lays out the do-re-mi. I shrieked, "But tit doesn't mean anything!" I was at a friend's house at the time, veins popping in my reddened neck, when her

little three-year-old daughter and budding anger-manage-
ment counselor tugged at my sleeve and quietly said,
"Please use your inside voice."

The violent fantasies have abated some. I was in danger
of becoming as rabid as any Clinton hater after several par-
dons and some light vandalism. You stole the Ws off our
computers. You stole the election. Nyah nyah. There I was
whining about feeling disenfranchised, powerless, bush-
whacked, and bewildered to a friend who is African American and she gave me a "how do you like it?" look that had
the effect of hysteria-stopping, cold-water slap in the face.
I have ramped down a notch.

But unlike some, I still find W's charm offensive. The
penchant for nicknaming and thus charming and dis-
arming the suckups we call the press has been widely and
warmly reported. Marc Lacey, of *The New York* "Hey Gray
Lady!" *Times,* lovingly reported that in a big-time display of
Texas-style levity and folksiness at a meeting of lawmakers
in Austin before the coronation, W called "a rather bulky
Democrat from California" name of Rep. George Miller,
"Big George."

The guy is brilliant! Unlike so much else in this beyond
teflon saga, the name stuck. And from now on, you better
be fixin' to call Fred Upton, a Michigan Republican,
"Freddy Boy" because that's what W dubbed him.

No one seems to take the double takes from the nick-
named as stunned horror that our "president" is indeed a
sophomoric, glad-handing frat boy. Or that his behavior is
akin to a pathetic plea for approval from the lowly office

guy who replaces toner and feels compelled to add "meister" to surnames. I mean no offense to sophomores or office workers. I do mean insult to frat boys.

Watts, Representative of Oklahoma, is reported to have welcomed the whimsical name calling as a break from the lemon-sucking seriousness of governance.

Okay, Okie Man, Token Man, suck on these. Joe Biden—Plug Man. Spenser Abraham—Loser Man. Gail Norton—Watt's Up? John Ashcroft—Integrity Man. Donald Rumsfeld—Viagra Man and/or Missile Man. Condoleezza Rice—Dianna Grrl, the last of the Supremes. Jim Baker—Bull Connor without the Stetson. Alan Gimme Some Greens Man. Ari Fleischer—Arrogant Condescending Infuriating Snippy Spokes Man. Rod Paige—Voucher Man. George W.—he's the Edumacation president!! Extra for when and if W ever goes to the Middle East—Ariel Butcher Boy Sharon.

Hey this is fun!! I'm charmed. These Smiling Path guys are fun, maybe the next four years won't be so bad.

Especially now that I've formed "The Kate Clinton Full Gospel Choir and Liberation Army." We've got religion and now we want our federal funds!! Bow your heads and join me in prayer: "Our father who art in Kennebunkport, please watch over the health of Dick Cheney, our old rugged boss. Our Lady of the Teleprompter, we know that when you move us to say "faith-based" you mean "you're on your own now, sucker." Thou who hast worked Supreme miracles in the past as recently as December, and who knows that the grievous sound we hear is the wall between church and state come tumbling down, vouchsafe unto us enough vouchers to pay this month's gas bill until we too are delivered from this hell of bipartisanshit and are born again into that heavenly estate that will soon be untaxed." Can I get an amen?

(2001)

Flying Fickle Finger of Fate

THE OTHER DAY I WAS talking to John Ashcroft. Well, I was talking. He was listening. My girlfriend tells me not to flatter myself, but I swear sometimes I hear clicks on our phone line. You just know that some day it will be revealed that J. Edgar Ashcroft often enjoyed a good threeway. Anyway, I was telling my friend about an incident at the Lesbian Health Conference.

While attending in Washington, D.C., two lesbians were standing in their hotel room window watching the world go by. Suddenly the Bush presidential motorcade roared by. Back from a run? Off to the ranch? Late for a war?

The two women were perhaps still miffed that the Bush administration's Health and Human Services had slashed $75,000 in conference funding just three months prior to the conference. For whatever reason and there are so many to chose from, they flipped the bird in the direction of the tinted windows of the Pres-mobile.

Faster than you can say or feel "a heightened state of alert," there was a knock on their door. It was fifteen minutes. Two burly Secret Service men entered the room and began questioning them. Shockingly unaware of the universal meaning of the flipped bird, the agents asked, "What did you mean by the gesture?" After the SS men left murmuring into their wristicuffs, the D.C. Metro police arrived to question the two women. After those uniforms left, the hotel security questioned them.

The night I thought I heard some clicks on my phone, my friend and I were wondering how the suits located the digit dykes so quickly. Where were the surveillance cameras? Was is it another tip from the hardworking people at Shoney's? Shouldn't the agents have been out looking for that white or black, young or old, civilian or military sniper in a perhaps/definitely white van? Maybe the middle finger gesture was just a friendly reminder from two health conscious lesbians to schedule another executive colonoscopy? How far did Cher turn back time? Pre-feminism? Pre-magnon? Pre-preemptive?

There are so many bird-flipping opportunities.

Donald Rumsfeld, Secretary of Offense, has let lapse the charter of The Defense Advisory Committee on Women in the Services [DACOWITS]. The respected volunteer agency, founded in 1951, had been instrumental in promoting gender integration in the military and, most recently, in promulgating the enlightened notion that lesbian -baiting is harmful to all women and to troop morale in general. If the group is ever rechartered, Rummy with the support of the Heritage Foundation, has limited its focus to recruitment, retention, and family issues. One Armed Services Committee member objected to gender-integrated basic training saying, "I don't think that the hand that rocks the cradle should be shooting at the heads of the enemy." I don't think the hand that flips the bird on this one should be slapped.

You'd never know it from the daily sports pages, but this is the thirtieth anniversary year of Title IX, the 1972 law requiring colleges to grant equal financing and resources to male and female athletics. With women's enrollment on the rise, colleges are scrambling to comply, not by increasing women's programs, but by slashing men's programs like wrestling and gymnastics (not men's football or basketball, you unpatriotic dummy). George Bush, Texas Ranger and Longhorn, has vowed to look into the law and to adopt a "reasonable approach" to enforcement. Preparations are being made for a pre-emptive strike on the University of Connecticut's Women's Athletic Department.

At a recent United Nations conference on children, the United States made a big axis of itself and joined with Iran, Libya, Pakistan, Sudan and the Vatican to oppose any language that supported the use of condoms in stopping the spread of AIDS. The message from the deputy secretary of HHS is, "We need to have very strong messages for young people and that is the message of abstinence until marriage, that the only safe sex is no sex and a mutually monogamous relationship." There was no message for gay young people. The sound you hear is bird flipping.

When asked on one of his many fundraising junkets, I mean policy speeches, where Laura was—and we all wonder, she's so absent, she's more Aura than Laura—George quipped that she was home getting the house ready for company, sweeping off the porch. Everybody laughed. Maybe because they knew it wasn't true. They all knew she makes Condoleezza do the sweeping.

I've got to start wearing mittens.

(2002)

Hormoneland Security

I LIKED GEORGE BETTER WHEN he was just reading to the kids, as was his former photo-op wont. But now he's reading to the grown-ups, and it's not a pretty sight. He gives pep talks that make the market tank by the end of the day. He shows up with the big "I care" messages splayed on the backdrop like scrolls of tacky ethical wallpaper: "Corporate Responsibility," "Homeland Security," "War on Terror." The words look as if they are going in one of his ears and out the other. In his programmed speak and spiel, he chants, "Malfeance! Gimme an M! Gimme an A! . . . What's that spell? No, really, what's that spell? What's it mean?"

In his address to Wall Street, he did not look good. He read his solutions for corporate mal-whatever. Double the incarceration for mal-doers who will never be incarcerated anyway. Bring on the SEC SWAT teams (as if!). When all else fails, invade Iraq and impeach Bill Clinton again.

At a press conference the day before, reporters had asked him direct questions, and that was frustrating for the poor guy. His brow was more furrowed than a Westminster sharpei, and a bucket of Botox couldn't smooth it out.

When the emperor has to wear clothes, don't make him wear that black and white moral houndstooth. It's really hard to be President, case you didn't know. Blame it on Karen. She left, and everything went to smash.

A little perspective, please. Whitewatergate started as an investigation of a $100,000 land deal—chump change to the curb!—and ended $50 million later with impeachment proceedings. But this financial scandal is much bigger. There's blow jobs, and there's snow jobs. And right now, we're snowed under.

But don't hold your breath waiting for the Democrats to capitalize on this scandal. Where is the Democrat's Ken "Jean Valjean" Starr? Please put away that eyebrowless Dick Gephardt. I swear if the Dems got hold of a picture of George drunk, naked, going down on Ari Fleischer in the Lincoln Bedroom with Dick Cheney at the door selling tickets to watch, they would not know what to do with it.

Interestingly enough, the disclosure of the fraudulent "restatement of earnings" coincides with discovery of the deleterious "replacement of hormones." The good news is that the Women's Health Initiative did urge women to stop taking the combo progestin/estrogen when it became clear that it was harmful to their health. Big Pharma be damned. The bad news is that six million women could be easing off their hormones in the next few weeks. Did somebody say SWAT teams?

Because I love my country, I humbly offer myself as head of the Office of Hormoneland Security. Unless, of course, the very gracious guru of women's health, Dr. Susan Love, who had warned about hormone replacement treatment for years, wants the job. Note that she is gracious enough not go around gloating, "I told you so."

We pledge to unmedicalize every menopausal symptom and make it work for the body politic.

Osteoporosis? Weight-bearing exercise such as walking has been shown to stem bone loss. Sounds like marching to me. We'll do the heavy lifting. Insomnia? Our SWAT teams will be on duty night and day for you.

Hot flashes? Our uniforms will be cotton, multilayered. The lights on our data-mining helmets will be auto-powered.

Forgetfulness? You wish. We'll Madame DeFarge our lists, and we will not forget.

Mood swings? Who wouldn't be cranky with the lack of sleep and hot flashes? We will be righteously angry and outspoken in a cautious, passive world.

Vaginal dryness? In a world of Viagra, you ain't seen anger yet.

To the Hormoneland!

(2002)

Emergency Preparedness

First, a few disclaimers: I love my country. I hate what's happening. I'm for peace. Since when did saying you are for peace, get translated into, "I think I'll have that darling Saddam over for dinner"? Is that a French translation? I support the troops. In this economy, it's good to know some people have found work.

Here at home, the war mission creeps into daily life. After three Kafkaesque days on the phone with various Verizon service representatives, I began to refer to them as "The Evil Empire," even though some of my friends are embedded in that corporation. In nightly life, FYI, a good foreplay line is not, "But, honey, whatever happened to that coalition of the willing?"

In my relationship, I have noticed a creeping unilateralism. I'm not proud of it. My forward leaning posture says, "Because I said so." And I have come to believe that if I repeat anything enough times, it becomes, perforce, true. Paula Zahn said we're winning. Paula Zahn said we're winning. . . .

My governmentally sanctioned my-way-or-the-high-wayism is an excuse for all kinds of bad behavior. I nod yes, yes, yes and then do whatever I damn well please. How do you think we got a couch in "Patrician pumpkin?" "Why did you buy that couch?" "God told me to." "We cannot afford it." "Trust me, deficit spending is good." "Why that color?" "May I remind you we are in an orange alert?"

I had stonewalled my dear partner for weeks on our operational readiness prep, but as the MSNBC countdown clock ticked down to just how far Cher turned back time, I relented and we followed the orders of Homeland Security Bear, Tom Ridge. And they say women are hysterical.

To quell the "@#$% duct tape?" backlash, Tom had appeared in what looked like an old cardigan from Jimmy Carter, and urged people to go to Ready.gov for their instructions. That's great for "we the people" who own computers, but it leaves out a large part of the truly unwired population. With some string and tin cans from the three days' supply of stored food, they can make a phone! If they only knew they were supposed to.

Ridge also said we should talk to our families and return to normal. That leaves out a large part of the gay population whose families have not talked to them in years and who have always had a problematic relationship with "normal." Though not the HBO movie with—yum—Jessica Lange.

According to Ready.gov, to get our preparedness mojo up to code, we had to do two things. First, pack two kits, one for home and one for travel. Second, make a plan to communicate with friends and family in an emergency.

Well, there's nothing like planning your emergency phone tree or packing an Armageddon outta-here kit to highlight your priorities. It's one thing when "If you could bring one thing out of a burning house, what would it be?" is a fun parlor game. [Hint: The fire.] But when you're living in a worst case-scenario handbook, your own unreality show, it's a kick in the gut.

However, since my galpal and I travel so much, we are seasoned frequent packers. If worst comes to worst, stick near us. Chances are, if I don't have what you need in my dop kit, my girlfriend does.

Basically, in our home kit, we have enough water and canned goods for three days, and of course, a lot of batteries. I insisted we also have as many Skinny cow silhouette bars in the freezer as will fit next to the bottle of vodka. Our emergency plan is to do whatever it takes to get back together and begin drinking the vodka.

Because that loud sucking sound you hear is the bombalicious Donald Rumsfeld draining any treasury he can to support his habit, gay orgs among others are in dire fundraising straights. A sure sign is the sad state of post-benefit-dinner goody bags. After a recent fundraiser, my goody bag contained a sample lemon Pledge-saturated dust mitten and a picture of some Manolo Blahnik shoes. Who could run for cover in those shoes anyway?

Hey, here's a thought: An enterprising gay organization

could combine goody bags and emergency kits for gay people. Isn't that a funny premise? Ha-ha-ha, whoo-ee. Evian water for three days!! Kiehl's new exfoliant for the quagmire. Zany, huh? And it is all dust in my mouth. Especially when I look at the names on my emergency phone tree: my dear friends, cherished gay family. The tree roots go deep and are entwined with the roots of the terrified Iraqi people, all precious beyond measure and I have no punch line.

(2003)

CULTURE WAR BRIDE

ALL THE GOOD NEWS AT the end of June highlighted just how bad the news has been. The Supreme Court upheld Affirmative Action at the University of Michigan. And while the Supreme Commander was still trying to strike down Saddam, the Supreme Court struck down sodomy. The whole thing almost made up for helping to steal that presidential election in 2000. But not quite. At all.

Prior to the Supreme stunner, the Ontario Court of Appeals had ruled that the exclusion of gays from the institution of marriage is "illogical, offensive and unjustifiable." Oh, Canada. I could drink a case of you. Then Michael Savage of MSNBC's Savage Nation told a caller/sodomist, "You should only get AIDS and die, you pig." The good news: MSNBC fired him, but then congratulated itself too mightily.

The Supreme's decisions were all too much for the supremacist, Strom Thurmond. And it was way too much for Pat Robertson. In "Operation Supreme Court Freedom," he took a prayerful contract out on certain Supreme Court Justices. They remained unnamed, but the congregation was given ailment hints: "one is 83 years old, one has cancer, one has a heart condition." The Don of the 700 Club closed his eyes and prayed discretely, "Would it not be possible for God to put it into the minds of these judges to retire?"

A week later, at the dedication ceremony for the opening of the Constitution Museum in Philadelphia, the Rev. Shar-pei almost got his mojo working. When the Justices pulled streamers to drop the scrim in front of the Constitution, a support beam dropped instead and was almost put into the brain of Sandra Day O' Swing Vote. Antonin Scalia was conveniently in another section of the museum at the time. Sadly, sassy Ann Coulter was off touring her book about the good old days of McCarthyism.

The 6 to 3 Sodomy decision, which incidentally Bill Bennett lost a bundle on because he picked Scalia at 5 to 4, featured that Axis of Egos: Rehnquist, Thomas and Scalia. Thomas, who had dissented in the Affirmative Action case because he did not want anyone else to experience the catastrophic success he's had to endure, dismissed the Texas sodomy law as "silly." That left the real vituperation to Scalia.

The Scalia of Justice did not disappoint. He railed that the decision was nothing more than a victory for the gay agenda in the ongoing culture wars and was dismayed that it would lead to gay marriage. That activated Trent's stunt double, Dr. Bill Frist, to threaten a new constitutional amendment, "The Marriage Limitation Amendment" i.e., marriage is between one man and one woman and she shall be submissive unto him and make her loins available to him every day. Sixteen words he did not add. Since when is the mere use of the word count function in the tool bar considered investigative journalism?

I'm no America Frister, yet it has taken me a long time to warm to same sex marriage. One of the cool things about being gay was that you didn't have to get married. Instead of trying to get the right to marry, I thought we should have been going around trying to talk ungay people out of it. If marriage is so natural, why the need for its constant defense, the elaborate ceremonies, the marriage benefit, the tax credits for children? It's as if those old Scared Straight programs have morphed into Paid Straight programs. A piquantly timed *Newsweek* cover on marriage painted a bleak picture of same old sex unions. Perhaps it's a conspiracy. If you want gay people to stop having sex, have them get married.

While I do believe gay people are entitled to every right and ritual straight people sort of enjoy, we have opted for the short form. As if cosigning monster mortgage payment papers were not commitment enough, my partner and I recently became Domestic Partners in the State of New York. She used to be my unindicted coconspirator, now she's my cultural war bride. We are registered at Target. In a simple ceremony at City Hall, next to the window where you could register to be a lobbyist, we paid twenty dollars for our papers. That's ten dollars less than a marriage certificate, but we do get fewer perks. Because of our new status, I am entitled to visit my d.p. in jail. Given that the Republicans are going to hold their convention a few blocks from our apartment, that is a very attractive feature.

(2003)

MEN BEHAVING BADLY

IN LATE AUGUST, MAJOR PHARMACEUTICAL companies began a full frontal publicity campaign for their new Viagra spin-offs. Apparently, men had been having a hard (or not-so-hard) time synching their Viagra four-hour window of opportunity with their dating, which could last five or six hours. Barring traffic jams.

To ease this crushing time-management problem, one new Viagra variant lasts thirty-six hours. It's called Cialis, which is Latin for "long weekend." Thirty-six hours? So much for Homeland Security. Get out that duct tape again.

In more unfortunate timing, the Gap people have just reintroduced their classic flat front chinos. Dockers will soon introduce pants with eight front pleats called Cockers. Sansibelts is thinking of unveiling Alta-Cockers.

Then came the news that male boomers are getting shot up with testosterone to stave off erectile dysfunction, loss of libido, and bouts of depression. The constellation of symptoms is known to some as andropause, the male version of menopause. Like early hormone replacement therapy for women, the bimonthly testosterone-replacement therapy (TRT) for men has unknown long-range health effects. Nevertheless, nearly 1.3 million prescriptions were written in the first six months of 2003. Bring it on!

But such therapy may not be enough. Men seem to be facing a relentless loss of potency at a very basic genetic level. Biologists have determined that the Y chromosome has been shedding genes for some evolutionary time now. As a result, it is a fraction of the size of its partner, the X chromosome. Mother Nature has barred the Y chromosome from the standard genetic swap meet called recombination, otherwise the Y chromosome would sneak into the X, making everyone male. Hey, you can't blame the Old Splice Girl. (All this was detailed in an article in *The New York Times,* post-Howell Raines, so it must be true.) Denied the benefits of recombining with the X, the helical strand of Y has been forced to survive by making a hairpin turn and recombining with itself. The sentence in Nicholas Wade's "Science Times" article that jolted me more than my morning java was, "This narcissistic process . . . seems to be what has saved men from extinction so far."

Now I know why men are narcissistic!

Whenever we read the paper or turn on the news these days, we see male narcissism on display: arrogant self-importance and entitlement, haughty lack of empathy, grandiose fantasies of power and security, and vengeful reaction to criticism.

Here are some prime specimens:

Joe Lieberman, freshly dipped in Betadyne for the Democratic debates, looks expectantly for a reward for his poco de Spanish. Meanwhile, he, Kerry, and Gephardt, feeling unappreciated, gang up on Howard Dean, who dares to run against the DLC.

Wesley Clark, fresh from map pointing in the CNN studios, announces his candidacy in his home state of Manchuria, while old Gore guys swarm behind him in Angela Lansbury drag.

Hummeroid *Arnold Schwarzenegger* disses Arianna Huffington while claiming he does not now and never has dissed women, much less pawed or groped.

Michael "Uday" Powell, head of the FCC, whines that the defeat of his proposal for new media ownership rules was caused by a "concerted grassroots effort to attack the commission from the outside in," which used to be called democracy.

Donald Rumsfeld, wearing his Alta-Cockers, sneers at every reporter's question, before spinning a globe to see where to invade next.

Karl Rove, now on the hot seat, may yet have to claim he overdosed at his TRT session in July as an excuse for the trashing of Ambassador Wilson and his wife.

Then there's *W.* at the U.N. Apparently, the Occupier-in-Chief did not get the reality show memo about what poor form it is to call someone irrelevant and then return a few months later and demand cash. That might be how they date in Texas, but those so-called chocolate makers in Old Europe are not having it.

(2003)

THE GAY CRAWL

·   ·   ·

Coming out is still the basic building block of the gay movement. Not the understood, wink wink, nudge nudge coming out. Not openly closeted. Saying it. The words—"Yep, I'm a lesbian." "I'm gay." The world might be a better place if straight people had to come out. A National Walk a Mile in Our Squarepants Coming Out Day. It changes everything. Not that that's a bad thing. Then saying it again. To self. To family. To friends. To children. To co-workers. And again, until you are sick of it. Until it sounds silly. Until you're good at it. So good you are living out and stepping out of our gayted communities. It is time for a second coming out, to challenge the silence of our so-called liberal friends. The continued tolerant/virulent reaction to homosexuality is a sign of end stage heterosexuality as we know it. Coming out speeds up the process. Bring it on.

I'll Laugh Tomorrow

IT MUST HAVE BEEN A LATE-CENTURY case of
P.T.E.S.S. (a.k.a. post-traumatic Ellen stress syndrome),
with its attendant classic symptoms—memory loss (inability
to remember gay history before Ellen came out), dissocia-
tion (inability to associate with gay organizations, tendency to
dis them, e.g., "Why should I join? Ellen is gay. It's O.K."),
addictive behavior (gin-drinking, obsessive long-distance
bike riding), depression (inability to get out of one's bed
and into another's)—that made it difficult for *The Advocate* to
imagine in its thirtieth anniversary issue the future of gay
humor. (In fact, the subject of gay humor may well have
seemed inappropriate for such a serious look at the future.)
But I have thought about it and hope to "stand in the gap,"
to borrow a phrase from the Promise Creepers.

Since the past serves as a prologue to the future, let's

look at the last thirty years of lesbian and gay humor, after a brief first look at what's happened to other minority humor, for hints of what is to come.

The humor of both the African-American culture and the Jewish culture was originally the humor of survival, a general pool of inside jokes that kept people going while on the plantation and in the ghetto. Since even oppressed people get busy, they had to hire one person who was very good at making fun of the Man. At the Apollo, in the Catskills. Then along comes the Man, who's heard all the laughing and feels left out, and he puts the comic on TV or hires him to write sitcoms. The joker for hire is smart enough to know he can't keep his job by continuing to make fun of his employer, so he makes fun of himself. That's when he gets the big bucks. Maybe even a Grammy or an Oscar. Then he's just like everybody else, has a place at the table up in the big house.

Our humor parallels the history of other minority humor—a shared pool of buoyant inside jokes, with paid practitioners always in danger of co-optation by mainstream media. The two strands of gay and lesbian humor became entwined in the mid-eighties in response to the right wing and the AIDS crisis, but prior to that the forms and context of gay and lesbian humor kept them separate. Gay men's humor was usually cabaret, piano bar, drag-oriented, bitchy camp with an emphasis on outfits, the big show, female. Lesbian humor was more traditional, individual, nonmusical, comedy club, tailored, stand-up, male. These male and female strands merged when lesbians and gay men began to appear together at fund-raisers, benefits, and march rallies. Lesbians put together more of a show, and gay men started to craft more traditional comic routines. Access to comedy clubs, with the promise of a vaunted six-minute spot on late-night talk shows, also served to recalibrate lesbian and gay humor. After Ellen DeGenerMorgan came out, the possibility of gays on TV and in movies held out promise to lesbian and gay comics of big bucks and big time.

While I wish that future humor will be the humor of change and challenge of the status quo, I fear that the conservatizing influence of the voracious maw of media and entertainment could prevail. The net effect of the Internet is to blur that ironic margin, to open a secret trapdoor in the back of the closet behind the shoe boxes, where gay cyberians can escape to the secret cybergarden beyond where there is no gender or orientation. The more our movement becomes a market, a niche just waiting to be scratched, the more our humor is reduced to lines on a bar code indicating "Laughs three times per minute at references to menstrual pads, icked out by mucous references, can't go beyond 'the vice president is dull' in political references."

If gay and lesbian comics take the easy road and speak only to that level of audience, all that will be left of our humor tradition will be Catskill hypnotists or the voices behind some family-oriented cartoon character—"See, the nice lesbian, honey? Don't be scared. Here's your action figure." The content of our humor will be, "Take my significant other, please"; "So on their wedding night, one dyke says to her wife . . ."; "Knock, knock. Who's there? Jodie. Jodie who? Just kidding."

(1997)

Scaring Them Straight

WHEN I SAW THE EXODUS International full-page ad in *The New York Times* TOWARD HOPE AND HEALING FOR HOMOSEXUALS, my first thought was that it must not be going well for conservatives if they have to throw away good money to advertise for straight people. All those institutions—marriage, churches, the military, schools—aren't doing their job, I guess.

My next thought was, "This is my country on drugs."

Friends of mine were dismayed, but I was thrilled. No more whisper campaigns. Let's get it all out in the open.

My eighty-nine-year-old father is always a bit skeptical when I describe the forces ranged against lesbians and gays. But with meteorologist Pat Robertson, Trent "Twelve-Stepping" Lott, and now Exodus, I've got evidence.

Their poster girl is Anne Paulk, wife (graciously submitting to her ex-gay husband, I hope, unless he wants to go to Disneyworld), mother, and former lesbian. Paulk says that when she was four years old, a teenage boy molested her. That eventually made her a lesbian, she says, but only God can make a tree. And instead of going to Exodus International, wouldn't Anne have been better served by a "Society for the Prevention of Cruelty to Little Girls?"

Despite the lesbian community's six degrees of separatism, no one I know dated Anne in college, where she says her sexual attraction to women blossomed with the help of the campus gay/lesbian group. Note to gay/lesbian campus groups: You're in for a rough year.

In the ad, Anne bows to Reggie White and Angie and Debbie Winans. She says when she was living as a lesbian she hated to hear prominent people refer to her life as a sin. For a second there I thought she was going to say "So I joined my local lesbian SWAT team and staged a sit-down strike in the editorial offices of our paper until they agreed to more balanced coverage of gay issues." But no. Instead, she had a leap of faith and "realized that God's love was truly meant for me." Through a Christian woman, herself a former lesbian, Anne says she was led to Exodus International, and their ministry helped her to overcome her homosexuality.

The ad does not say what steps the program took to scare her straight. Cattle prods? Pictures of J. Edgar Hoover in taffeta? De-affirmation tapes that warned, "You're going to have to play catcher on your softball team until you're eighty"?

Clever that the first ad in the TRUTH CAN SET YOU FREE campaign used a woman. We're not so threatening, we're fickle (I'm a lesbian—oh, never mind), and guys need us in marriage to procreate and make casseroles.

The ad ended with a plea that if you're gay or know someone who is gay, call this number. The number was wrong, and callers reached a baffled electrician in Alabama. New Yorkers were amazed that an electrician was home to answer his phone.

Update: Two days after the Exodus International ads appeared, a coalition of gay and lesbian groups took out their own ads in *USA Today* and *The New York Times.*

I was proudly dismayed. Proud that we had responded in a timely fashion, but dismayed that it has come to this. Would that we could so quickly raise that money to fund gay teen groups or school counseling programs instead of funneling it into our own versions of JUST DO IT, THINK DIFFERENT, CROSS DRESS FOR LESS.

Next up for ex-gay ads: HATE THAT GAY? WASH IT AWAY!

(1998)

Diagnosis: Lesbian

THE FOLLOWING ARE INDICATIONS OF the state of women's health research at the end of the century (note, not the eighteenth century): In a study of hypothalamus size and its correlation to homosexuality, a researcher stated that he had no data about lesbians because he was unable to locate any lesbian brains. I've been to that bar, too.

Some researchers have suggested that one of the best ways to reduce the risk of breast cancer is to remove both healthy breasts.

Viagra seemed to get FDA approval in about 20 minutes—*"Does Bob like it? Well, O.K., let's roll 'em out!"*—whereas women have been trying to get RU486, which we are going to need now more than ever, into this country for about 120 years.

In this context of women's health in general and lesbian health in particular, how cheering it is to welcome the first student study on lesbian health from the Institute of Medicine! The goal of the study, *Lesbian Health: Current Assessment and Directions for the Future* (to order it yourself, log on to http: www.nap.edu), is to address the entire scope of lesbian health in the community and to let mainstream America know that gay health is not only about HIV, the virus that causes AIDS.

In summarizing the many disparate, smaller studies of lesbian health, the report confirms that lesbian health is not generally different from women's health. But that is complicated by the added dimension of homophobia. The more a lesbian conceals her identity, the more susceptible to depression and aches and pains she becomes. Because lesbians have fewer children than heterosexual women, they are more at risk for certain kinds of cancer. Because lesbians may cope with environmental homophobia by increased smoking and drinking, they are more at risk for heart disease.

The study also lays the groundwork for future efforts. Since lesbians face unique challenges from an alternately homo-ignorant and homophobic medical establishment, the report recommends the creation of health care facilities that tailor services to lesbians as well as the education of mainstream doctors, hospitals, and researchers about the concerns of lesbian patients.

I'm not a doctor; I don't even play one on TV. I did play doctor when I was eight with my friend Desiree *near* a TV. But based on my examination of lesbians over the years, I

humbly offer some almost-scientific observations and rec-
ommendations for further investigation:

Just because the word *HMO* looks like *Homo* doesn't mean
it offers good health care for lesbians. Generally, the
inverse is true.

The so-called DeGeneresative Syndrome needs further
research. This is the mistaken notion that the lights have to
be on and cameras rolling with Barbara Walters waiting
expectantly on your living room settee in order for you to
come out.

The phenomenon of Menstrual Amnesia needs further
study. How can a detail-oriented young woman forget from
one month to the next that she's going to get her period,
despite all the signs? *Backache? Must have done too many sit-ups.
Breasts tender? Too many push-ups. Blood on the couch? Must have cut my
leg shaving.*

The new, much-anticipated Viagra for women needs
more testing. It can cause blushing, painfully erect nipples
and wide-ons. If one is experiencing sexual dysfunction,
perhaps it's time for a new partner.

The new PMS, i.e., Post-Monica Stress syndrome, needs
investigation. Disassociation, depression, and an unnatural fondness for Altoids-enhanced fellatio are rampant
among former C-SPANaholics who now have too much
time on their hands.

Further study on sleep deprivation in new lesbian
mothers as it affects local organizing needs to be done. In
a related area, further investigation is needed on ACWC
(Adult Children Without Children) groups and their long-
term abandonment issues.

It is also noted that while WNBA games, LPGA tournaments, Olivia Cruises, and Lilith Fairs do offer salutary health clusters, many a woman in attendance would otherwise not say "lesbian" even if her mouth were full of one. Progressive medical studies aside, the deleterious effects of the Openly Closeted Reflex are still pandemic.

(1999)

Ex-Gay Files

JUST AS THE *SPORTS ILLUSTRATED* Swimsuit issue is a sure sign that February is almost over, and the plastic grocery bag caught billowing in a bare tree is harbinger of Spring in the Northeast, the annual appearance of ex-gay ads are the new portent that summer is upon us. I never thought I'd miss seersucker.

When I saw the first ads which claimed, with the help of God's ministers, to retool gay people into, if not full-blown straight people then at least ex-gay people, I thought, "Gosh, it can't be going well for straight people, they have to advertise now."

Sponsored by the group Fuckus on the Family, the ads featured Ann and John Paulk, both so-called ex-gays. I was fascinated by Ann, a "former lesbian" and did some informal research in my travels. The lesbian population is not large. If you laid every lesbian end to end—what a weekend! My point is we know everybody's business; it's like six degrees of separatism. Everywhere I went I asked audiences if anyone present had dated or knew someone who had dated Ann, and there was never a hand with a shortened index finger raised. If we didn't know about her, I say she wasn't a lesbian in the first place.

This proselytizing season, as we await this year's ex-gay poster couple, and why do so many ex-gays date each other, we can read the new book, *Coming Out Straight* by Richard Cohen. Okay, WE don't have to read it—I read it for you.

Subtitled Understanding and Healing Homosexuality, the earnest tome has a foreword by the much aggrieved Dr. [of what?] Laura Schlessinger. Her screed against the monolithic agenda of homosexual activists made me wonder what united gay front I was missing. Her plucky exhortation that with the help of God and "some intestinal fortitude" many "gays" [sic] can change their lives if they chose to do so, made me want to wrap my bootstraps around her plucking little neck.

But like the nails, I pressed on. The author, Richard Cohen, who also successfully rid himself of his Jewish identity, was told when he was young that he was not ready to play Beethoven's *Moonlight Sonata,* so he just went out and bought the music and taught himself, dammit. And gay-sayers to the contrary, he says that with the help of a very handsome Jesus in his life, a long-suffering wife and male mentors who hugged him nonsexually, he healed from homosexuality. One can do it. And then one can leave one's job as part-time waiter/ballet manager, become a well-paid counselor/lecturer, head a foundation that preys on tortured gay people, make a lot of money, and put an addition on the house, he did not add.

In an early bracketed disclaimer, Cohen announces that "instead of saying HE and SHE each time, I will use the masculine pronoun." He is a busy guy and those extra esses slow him down. Midst snappy flowcharts and impressively footnoted diagrams, we learn that no one is born homosexual, no one chooses to have same-sex attractions, anyone can choose to change, what was learned can be unlearned and my favorite "It's not gay nor bad, it's SSAD—Same-Sex Attachment Disorder." He claims that homosexuality, which he says does not exist, is in fact caused by heredity, temperament hetero-emotional wounds, homo-emotional wounds, sibling wounds, body image wounds, sexual abuse, social or peer wounds, cultural wounds, and "divorce/death/intrauterine experiences/adoption/religion." I thought you'd want to know.

Whenever I hear "ex-gay" I am reminded of one of my favorite Monty Python sketches. A man returns a parrot to the pet shop where he purchased it and tells the clerk, and I'm compressing hysteria here, "This parrot is dead. It is an ex-parrot." And the clerk argues, "He's not dead. He's pining." Coming Out Straight left me feeling SAD, filled as it with stories of ex-gays, not dead, despite attempted suicide and near-life experiences, but pining for peace with their desires and attractions. Even the glad news that the profoundly reactive ex-gay movement would not exist without an active gay movement is small consolation.

(2000)

GAY VAGUE

RECENTLY MY EYE WAS UNCHARACTERISTICALLY
drawn to *The New York Times* House and Home section. I generally flip past that section because the houses scare me.
Where do they keep their tweezers? But a picture with two
fancy, tuxedoed men and one woman in a black cocktail
dress walking through a manicured field, carrying cham-
pagne flutes and laugh laugh laughing, well gaily, stopped
me. The copy line read, "It's time for your crystal to come
out of the closet as well."

The accompanying article deconstructed this and other
ads as examples of a new cutting-edge genre called "Gay
Vague." The line about the closet in the Waterford crystal
oeuvre was cleverly used only in gay publications, which
seemed reverse to me. The ad for a swivel-top trash can,

"Swings both ways," was parsed. Another furniture ad with two fit, white men on either end of a white couch with a cherubic child on a child-sized chair in front of them, was said to cause perplexity in straight audiences who were confused by the triangulation, while it caused irresistible retail urges in gay audiences who then rose up as one, went out, bought a couch and a child. If I read the article right.

Gay Vague targets young gay bucks with big bucks who don't want to label themselves. The label-less state is dubbed "genderation inspecific." Even that is vague. It is really "orientation inspecific." In Google-researching this article, I was unable to locate any discussion on gay vague and bisexuality.

The *Times* article "When Intentions Fall Between the Lines" prompted a steamed column from Amy Holms in Voter.com. The Subaru ad, "It's not a choice. It's the way we're built," was as offensive to her as elephant dung is to others. She opined that the ads make straight people out to be dolts. She felt the ad for the Lesbaru was a not just a blatant pitch to the gay niche, but was also selling the notion that the straight, urban world is an enemy of liberation. Hey, we are not the ones buying the Humvees.

When Robert Kennedy—no, not that one—publisher of the upcoming *American Health and Fitness* wrote to potential advertisers that unlike others, he would not use those "debauched, wet-lipped men" who "look like they can be seduced" on his muscle covers, he outraged some gay activists and no doubt disappointed others. GLAAD's Scott Seomin said he thought Kennedy's message of the gay voyeur sets gay men up for discrimination and second-class treatment. It's no mean feat to distinguish one's health magazine in the racks and racks of them, so even talking against the gay vague type is a wily and free ad strategy. I know it prompted me to be on the lookout for the pasty featherweights in pinstripes on Kennedy's covers.

While for some ad people, gay vague is a strategy, for me, it is a perfect description of the unsettled feeling I've been having about my dear old gay movement. June used to be the month of Gay Liberation celebrations. After marathon, knock-down, drag-out committee fights, the words Lesbian, Bisexual, and Transgender were added. Then because all those words took up too much ad space and costly ink, it became the sandwich-sounding GLBT. In the past two Junes, all those hard-won words and letters have been dropped for the bland "Pride" brand. Gay Liberation marches have become Pride street fairs.

Ellen DeGeneres' coming out, though tasteful, was too unvaguely gay for people. Her show was canceled, because people could not allow it the time to be lesbian and funny. HBO, home of *Sex in the City*, which most of my gay men friends in true gender inspecificity, believe is about them, has brought Ellen back in a new hour special. She has not lost her ability to be wicked funny, but I wanted to hear that same smart specific humor turned on the details of her coming to coming out and its aftermath. The opening hilarious, though wordless dance was meant to represent that whole historical moment and I was left, like Tony Bennett in New York, feeling somehow sadly gay. I have faith she will get to those details in her new series.

Now rainbow decals and equal signs are wink wink,

nudge nudge brands meant to signify gay identity. Going to WNBA games [the new women's music festival], gay chat rooms [the new closet] gay cruises ["The only straits you'll see are Gibraltar!"] pass as political work. Consumerism as activism? I'm not buying it.

During the Republican Vague convention, bracketed by so-called Reality TV, Log Cabin Syrup Republicans announced hopefully that anti-ERA, anti-choice, pro-slavery number two, Dick Cheney, is a moderate because he and his wife have a lesbian daughter. They grant him humanitarian points for not disowning or having Mary committed to an ex-gay rehab. They gloss over Lon's "She did no such thing!" response to a question about Mary's coming out.

But heck, I'll be leaving the political comedy biz soon and returning to high school English teaching because, if I heard Dubya right, there is going to be big bucks in education come November and I for one am not going to miss the money train this time around.

(2000)

THE GAY CRAWL

LEAPIN' BOTOX! WE'RE GOING TO have our own Gay Channel! All over town "Fantasy Gay TV Programmer" is the now party game. Everybody's playing! Naturally, I want my own late night show, Satellite Dish.

Before we get into a GLBT Studies discussion of the ins and outs of such a thing, let's do take a minute to revel. Before *Ellen*, *Will and Grace*, or *Queer as Folk*, all gay viewers could do was wait for Paul Lynde to be the round peg in his Hollywood Square, decode and deconstruct a Lily Tomlin special ["Look! She's wearing purple. Discuss!"] or decrypt PBS Where's Waldo-like programming to find "In the Life." Instead of gay TIVO, it's Gay TV.

Of course, if you watched with my girlfriend, you would be convinced that everyone on TV is already gay. Her constant commentary is, "He is so gay," or less often, "She's such a lesbian." Every weather man. Most quarterbacks. When John Madden squeals, "Look at him scramble out of the pocket," I get the nudge. *The Antiques Road Show? The Christopher Lowell Show?* Gay men telling us what to do with our stuff.

In our household, with the exception of that whining second-rate Canadian skating pair, the Salt Lake Olympics might as well have been called The Gay Winter Olympics. But they would have been sued. The breakup of the women's couple in the still called "two man bobsled" team? Dyke drama. "The luge is a very gay event," my viewing companion pronounced. Watching what look to me like high-speed sperm rattling down a crooked, slick chute, I ask, "How do you know that?" at the exact moment the announcer with the Vaseline over his mike intones, "She's controlling the whole thing with her inner thighs." Nudge.

Her "Name It and Claim It" viewing habit stems of course from her incorrigible ability to think the best of people. As persuasive as she sometimes is, I'm not buying it. TV is straighter and scarier than ever. Because of an unsettled economy, and decreased ad revenues, TV is forced to produce more shows on the cheap, except of course for the Friends who get a million each per episode. Hey, they are so worth it.

Survivor, Temptation Island, or the so-called reality genre, are really what interest straight people about themselves. One critic said that *The Chair* and *The Chamber,* the second genre-ation shows with their soupçon of S/M, tap into and defuse an undercurrent of anger in the country. So show them on Al-Jeezera. *The Chair,* mercifully canceled, was hosted by John McEnroe, torture enough. In *The Chamber,* a contestant is strapped in a chair, doused with hot and cold water and asked questions. *Guantanamo Bay Watch*? or a Thursday night down at The Big Cock? Welcome to *Gay Jeopardy*!

It's no wonder gay people want their own channel. Some gay cultural commentators have worried that a gay channel could have the effect of draining gay content from mainstream shows, thereby invisibilizing our hard-won visibility. Perhaps. The new gay channel could in fact be a safe haven away from really bad TV, a lab for development of investigative journalism, fearless questioning, open debate, hour-long dramas. I'll give it a will and grace period, but I ain't holding my lesbian breath.

In addition to Gay per View, we should purchase the crawl space on every TV bandwidth, that space at the bottom of the screen where the terror ticker tape has been running 24–7 since 9–11. That "down there" used to be just the province of financial networks. As Lou Dobbs jowled on about the wonders of Enron, you could read that your 401K was worth as much as your Levi 501s.

Now any channel worth its shares is scrolling. We'd run ours all the way around the screen, so you could read it while lying on your side. Like *Mystery Science Theater* without the silhouettes, our crawl would run dishy comments on whatever was on the screen. Dick Cheney making a rare appearance? "Father Knows Best." Greta Von's new eye job? "Her new FOX contract would not allow her to bring her old face from CNN." And it is a known scientific fact that when you are reading the crawl you cannot hear what is being said.

Let's roll!

(2002)

A Pain in the Apse

I DON'T KNOW ABOUT YOU, but this Gay Pride, I can't wait to see the Dignity float!

In years past, the Gay Catholic group lived up to its name and was like a prayerful moment of silence between the highly-amped, Zima-sponsored, bar floats and the mega-megaphoned, chanting, whooping affinity groups.

Many a blazing Sunday, standing under the mandatory billowing rainbow balloon arc, I have been asked by a fellow reveler who couldn't see what was going by on the parade route, "What happened? Did somebody's generator go down?" "No, I bet it's Dignity."

Long ago, after sixteen years of Catholic education and much to the chagrin of my daily-Mass-going, Irish Catholic mother, I renounced the Catholic Church and most of its works. I did not want to be in something that did not want me. From a very early age I sensed the hypocrisy of Christian dyslexia. They hated the sinner; they loved the sin, couldn't get enough of it. I had also come to believe that a spiritual idea that needs large buildings and expensive outfits to keep it going, is not all that spiritual.

But that was just me. I marveled at my Catholic gay friends in Dignity who continued their church-going and worked for change. Goddess bless them. I had little faith that change would come. But thanks to gay liberation, and in a shorter time than it took to pardon Galileo for suggesting the sun, not the Church, was the center of the universe, change is a-coming!

The cosmetic changes of Vatican II—feng shuiing the altar, strumming the hootenanny Mass, dropping the Latin—were mere spiritual Botox on the face of things. Gay liberation, which offered the possibility of living full, well-ordered, gay and lesbian lives had to have siphoned off many so-called "vocations" from the Church. But most important, and in this I have absolute faith, the courageous act of coming out of the closet, telling our truth with all the freedom it brings, is a spiritual act and it has had a quantum cultural effect. Those poor souls who lived for years with the secret of their abuse, compounded by the shameful, clerical cover-up, finally came out and spoke their truth. What's that sound I hear? Why, it's walls come a tumbling down.

Do we get any credit? Heck no, we are still a pain in their apse. The Pope called the U.S. cardinals to Rome for his Red Party. [Next stop for the Bishoprics Circuit Party? Lock up the altar boys, it's Dallas this summer!]

And even though he sounded like Cosmo Castorini in *Moonstruck*—"Idonwannatalkaboudit"—His Extreme Round-headedness did manage to say in his address, "Non Askium, Non Tellium," that homosexuality is a disorder and should be rooted out. After, in the slowest spin session ever, bald-headed cardinal after bald-headed cardinal condescendingly informed us, "You don't understand what celibacy is." No, Clothman, YOU don't understand what celibacy is.

The Vati-because-we-can is sending out doctrinal alb-blasters on "apostolic visitations" of U.S. seminaries, because as you know something like this would never ever happen in Poland, to bust up aggressive gay cliques and to evaluate "ecclesiastic flamboyance—a tendency to embrace stagier elements of the liturgy." In what parallel universe are ukulele Masses considered flamboyant?

Despite the predictable gay scapegoating, I had been wondering how long it would take to blame women for the whole mess. Faster than you can say "Mother Church," Gary Willis, in his examination of the scandal in *The New York Review of Books*, coolly points to the role of a priest's mother in the moral infantilization necessary to commit such crimes with such impunity. According to Willis, many boys became priests to satisfy their status-seeking mothers. Oh, I see, it's the pedestal, not the pedophilia.

We can all see the handwriting on the sanctuary wall: The backlash is coming. But meanwhile, let's celebrate! This gay pride season, if they'll give me a special dispensation, I'll be riding high on the Dignity float, celebrating the power of gay liberation. So far we've destroyed the military and the church. That's some powerful stuff. I'll be the one in the ball-fringed Papal Drag cut on the bias, with the bullhorn. Please come up and kiss my ring.

(2002)

The Ha Ha Sisterhood

LAST YEAR, AT A COLLEGE Pride celebration, I was introduced by the co-chair as a "Stonehenge lesbian." I think he meant Stonewall—but in an odd way the label fit. Except in obituaries, female comics are never accorded the "loveable old curmudgeon" encomium of a George Burns or Bob Hope. Still, I wear my Stonehenge pendant with pride. It may be a quaint artifact on frayed rainbow hemp, but it represents several generations of lesbian comics, many still making a living at it, some even able to buy things.

There may or may not be a lesbian comedy boom, but there certainly is a lescom circuit. Gay Pride Month, formerly known as June, is like a rolling trade show for us. We fan out across the country to emcee Pride rallies, perform at local benefits, and headline our own shows. While hosting mammoth fundraising dinners, we vamp when the videos go down, the vegetarian entrees are lost, or the main speaker is stuck in traffic. We perform at summer women's festivals and on Olivia cruises. Provincetown in the summer is the Branson of lesbian comedy—ask anyone who has been subjected to the daily beach leafleting.

These days, lescom nation has some very visible titular heads. Ellen—rehabilitated after her perfectly calibrated emceeing of the much-postponed post-9–11 Emmy Awards—is on the road doing sold-out shows. In many interviews she seeks to reassure audiences that her act is funny-funny, not funny-gay. She has said that, in prospective markets for her new talk show, TV station managers sit in her audience. "I don't think it's an audition so much as it is a reassurance that I'm not some big, scary, gay agenda woman."

Rosie O'Donnell, whose coming out was an awesomely staged campaign, did a reportedly hysterical set at a New York City fundraiser about the pressure she felt. That was before she made her big announcement. But in the mandatory post-coming out interview with Larry King, Rosie, too, sought to reassure audiences that she was funny-funny, not funny-gay. I worry that somewhere, some late-blooming lesbian will postpone coming out because she doesn't think she can do well on Larry King.

The reticence illustrates how limited the tolerance for actual lesbian humor—as opposed the laff-riot of porno "lesbians" with blond mullets, long fingernails, tongues flicking in the nipple area—remain, at least among mainstream producers.

In fact, straight audience are less homo-ignorant than the impresarios. Humor that shows lesbian are just like everyone else—they eat meat, too! they are searched at security, too!—is acceptable. But, while straight sexual humor skews from family vanilla to swinger blue, it will be a long Will-&-Grace period before lesbians can crack a dirty joke on network TV. And what goes for sex goes double for politics.

In most queer comedy lineups, gay men are outnumbered by lesbians—not because of any rule about gender parity. The entertainment industry affords many more opportunities for funny gay men to make a living. Lesbians are likely to be drawn to stand-up, if only because it's cheaper to produce and therefore more accessible for women. But the very form of stand-up—with its setup/punchline; up/down; tumescence/detumescence (where the classic "tum-de-dum" rimshot actually originated)—is masculine.

It's no accident that, in the queer gender-perverse universe, so many funny gay men are drawn to cabaret, piano bar, and drag-oriented, bitch, campy, big-outfit, big-show formats. The rejection of male power is serious business and the only way a man is allowed to do it is through the morphing vapors of non-threatening feminine drag. But lescoms are allowed to "poke" fun. Their embrace of the stand-up form is a rejection of the "privileges" and props of the feminine. The joke is no longer on them. The layers of double and triple entendres from this essential irony make lescoms bold, bad, and wickedly funny.

On any given night in any queer comedy showcase, you might see three generations of lescoms, the first doing material about the what of coming out, the second riffing on the so-what of living out in the world, and the third dealing with the now-what of the changing world we live out in. Robin Tyler was the first lescom to come out on national TV. Lea DeLaria, from the same generation as Marga Gomez and me, kicked the closet door wide open on Arsenio Hall. Although DeLaria concentrates on her singing and acting career, her between-songs patter is still often trenchant, smartass lesbian humor.

Second-gen lescoms, who got their performance chops during the boom-boom Clinton years, are products of a less overtly oppositional time. With Clinton, a president who could say gay and lesbian without spitting up, many people came out, including a large number of lescoms. This allowed for much greater particularity, as in Suzanne Westenhoefer's material about her butch "homo depot" girlfriend; Vickie Shaw's material about living out as a divorced, Southern ex-fundamentalist raising three kids; and Karen Williams's pointed humor about being an African American single lesbian mother.

Julie Goldman, a brawny, brainy butch, is a next-generation lescom. Her edgy, urban humor is about being a young lesbian with no money temping in an office of straight women in a post-9–11 world of hidden cameras and nuclear threats. Goldman, who fronts a mock rock band called Indigo Etheridge, makes a creative community of next-gen comics, such as Jessie Kierson and Mary C. Matthews, in her hilarious short films.

Lesbian humor is uniquely good precisely because it's not in the mainstream. Since it isn't trying to sell anything, it doesn't have to sell out. Coming out as a lesbian onstage is still a very political act; if it weren't more women would do it. Speaking as a lesbian against the current feminist backlash has that same sense of danger—job loss, family and friend estrangement, violence—that it had 30 years ago. It's the biggest, scariest agenda of all.

(2002)

What the L?

THE SAME WEEK *THE L-WORD* premiered on Show-time, The W announced that he was going to press for $1.5 billion for his so-called "Healthy Marriage Initiative." More cry-for-help than policy, the red meat thrown before the Atkins wing of The Republican Party [see also Mad Vow] would offer training to low-income couples in interpersonal skills that sustain healthy, read "straight," marriage—avoiding child care payments, cheating on one's spouse, and disposing of the body.

Kidding.

Actually the initiative would teach problem solving, negotiating, and listening, skills, which might then trickle up to the Bush administration. Advertising campaigns will publicize the value of marriage, augmented by the fine work of The Bachelorette and My Big Fat Fiancé. A mentoring program will use married couples as role models of healthy marriage. If you're thinking Britney and Jason, or Liza and David, you are being as condescending to marriage as this initiative is to poor people.

The L-word. The M-word. Coinky dink or causal? Preemptive or post-emptive? Also that week the Husband-in-Chief announced that he was going to press for funds for the "Pow You to the Moon Project," formerly known as "Star Wars Missile Defense." *The L-Word*'s original name had been *Earthlings* and the L's meet regularly at a local queer hangout called The Planet. Stop me before I connect more dots. Well, they couldn't call it Neverland could they?

They could have, because most of us older L's NEVER thought we'd see *The L-Word* on television. Our household signed up for Showtime, no doubt sinking me and my cultural war bride in a Homeland Security counterinsurgency data mine somewhere.

I have every confidence that given more of a chance than Ellen ever got, the show will develop character and story lines to rival any long-running soap opera. We enjoyed the first episode. It's been a very cold winter in the Northeast so we appreciate the heat potential of the weekly series and the savings on our home heating bill.

I also enjoyed the foreplay of the previews and the post-coital cigarette reviews. Some previews said the show was a soft porn, "Lesbian Thigh for the Straight Guy." Most reviews opined that the show was not reflective of lesbian life. Repeat after me—Tel-e-vi-sion.

For a few days after the first episode I viewed my own life through an *L-Word* lens. Me at the dry cleaners—"This would be a great scene," and fantasized that the character of the young Shane, the sexual roué, was based on my life. Finally, my domestic partner kindly pointed out that I am an actual lesbian. Still there are a few episodes I would like to see.

WHAT THE L?

During an intake exam when they finally go to the sperm bank, Jennifer Beals discovers through a background DNA check that she is the great-great-granddaughter of Strom Thurmond. Should she come out about it? She tells one L and soon the whole alphabet knows. She rends her T-shirt in shame and restarts a trend. All the L's rally around her, don short spiky orange wigs and welcome her to the hangout with the banner "Nous Sommes Toutes Les Filles de Strom Thurmond."

THE L-BOAT: A Navy of Ex-Lovers Cannot Sail

The L's all go on a lesbian cruise together to celebrate the franchising of The Planet. While at sea, a friend of bisexual Alice, who is dogsitting her pitbull/poodle mix, accidentally trips the invisible electric dog fence which shuts down the California power grid, which trips the terror color levels to orange, so Gov. Col Klink authorizes the Coast Guard to board the ship. The L's are in the middle of a Mistress and Commander shipboard game, mistakenly think the Coasties are part of the game and attack them with pool noodles. They impound the ship and toss all the L's into Guantanamo until further notice. Ginger, the prison warden, has pity on them.

L HATH NO FURY

An ex-lesbian turned rogue Christian fundamentalist reparative therapist and hair dresser named Ann Paulk starts hanging out at the Planet leaving pamphlets, talking Bible trash and trying to repair Shane's sexuality and/or her Keith Richard's hair style. Talk about stalking!! The Ls get wind of her nefarious plans and decide to do some deep psych op on her. First, Alice checks her extensive lesbian family tree/burning bush and finds no mention of Ann anywhere. If the Ls never did her, she was never a lesbian! Their planned exposé goes awry when Shane reaches for some NutraSweet and seduces Ann by mistake. Later Shane credits Kate Clinton for the move.

AWOL

The Queer Eye for the Straight guys blow into LA to do the inevitable makeover of Tim, the unwittingly lesbian identified boyfriend of Jenny. It's like reparative therapy but different. They raze Jenny's writing studio and build him an inground wave pool and home gym. They make a chagrined Tim lose the Speedo and get him a thong. He starts hanging out in West Hollywood. Then it goes terribly wrong. They get him hooked on Crystal meth and circuit parties. He's never home. Marina moves in on Jenny. The Ls at the Planet [and at home] love Tim and get him into rehab and chase the fab five out of town.

WHEN L FREEZES OVER

Turns out blonde Tina's father is the Vice President of the United States! During the v-p debates, he had sidemouthed that the whole issue of gay unions should be left to the states. He changes his tune and says he is in favor of a constitutional amendment to limit marriage to straight people. And he's coming to visit! The libber Ls are outraged for Tina and think she should not let him in the house. The conservative Ls feel her pain, but don't want her to upset him, what with his heart condition and all. After a prolonged body cavity search by her father's Secret Service detail, Vice Dad says wink wink, he didn't mean her. He's got people who will do nuptials in his private bunker/wedding chapel.

(2004)

It's Not the Heat, It's the Vapidity

•   •   •

For this chapter, and verse, God spoke directly through me! Holy spellcheck! Watch for the smotes and smites, the begats and bigots. The Reverend Father Bush always wears an I-GOD. He gives himself goosebumps when he homilizes against fanatic clerics running countries. Worldwide, the crisis in faith is a basic fundamentalist dyslexia: they love the sin; they hate the sinner. It is faith debased. Also, the husband shall have dominion over the wife and she will not get desperate. The church shalt protect fetuses more than they protect actual live children. A 2005-year-old Christian identity movement feels victimized by a 35-year-old gay identity movement. How in God's name? They dip in the Bible for answers. It's like Google for Christians. It is a faith accompli that religious security will be bankrupt by 2042. Religion is the opposite of the people.

Surprise! It's Evolution

HOLD THE PRESSES! BIG NEWS out of the Vatican. Almost 150 years after Darwin hypothesized that the human body might not be an immediate creation of God but a product of a gradual process of evolution, Pope John Paul II has announced through a spokesman that maybe Sir Charles was onto something. Honeys, I am breathless.

In a related story, Dignity, a national organization of gay and lesbian Catholics, added a Post-it to the papal announcement. "We also believe that the human body might not be an immediate creation of God except in the case of Greg Louganis or Martina Navratilova."

The Pope, still convalescing from his appendix operation, announced through a papal rep that "fresh knowledge leads to the recognition that the theory of evolution was more than just a hypothesis." Is that coy enough?

Whatever was in the papal phenobarbital?

Maybe the very mysterious "fresh knowledge" came to the Pope when he was under anesthesia. Or his in-room cable service was rerunning *Planet of the Apes.*

Of course, the Church has been trying to clean up its apse and get ready for the third millennium by amending the wrong teachings of the past. The hierarchy grudgingly copped to the fact that Galileo was right when he said that the sun, not the Earth, not even the Pope, was center of the universe. It took them seventeen years of study and a picture of a guy playing golf on the moon, but they did finally admit that they done Galileo wrong.

What's next? "Isaac Newton: Gravity, Who Knew?"

This is not the first time the Church has tried to grapple with the evolution question. In 1950, Pope Pius XII, a.k.a "The Shrunken Applehead Pope," cautioned the faithful, in the encyclical "Sui Generis," to regard Darwinism as a theory and not a doctrine. Then he died of the hiccups.

Surprise of all surprises. His Very Narrowmindedness did not go far enough in "Darwinius erat Correctus After Allus." Enough with the Homo Erectus, I would have appreciated a little more comment on the social Darwinism of this late century. Our National Selection Process cuts the weak out of the herd and makes him President. Rupert Murdoch, the Antichrist, has the most fits and survives.

In mid-October, I went to Washington, D.C., to be with my friends, living and dead, at the final full display of the Names Project AIDS Memorial Quilt. The Park Service police felt compelled to measure it in terms of football fields, hardly a proper unit of measurement for so many drag queens.

As happened to me at the previous display of the Quilt, after an hour of panel-searching, a head-down, sad-day-at-the-beach kind of shuffle, I became enraged. It could have been the facility next to the information tent called the "Wellness Pavilion" and sponsored, without apparent hint of irony, by the pharmaceuticals (Rausch handed out free Kleenex packs emblazoned with its name). It could have been the cappuccino. Or it could have been the debut of Red Ribbon Ale.

We're not a movement anymore; we've evolved. We're a niche market just waiting to be scratched.

(1996)

It's Not the Heat, It's the Vapidity

THEY CALLED THE SUMMER OF 2003 the Summer of Gays. I don't know who they are, but how do they manage to make it sound like 1977's Summer of Sam? Wait a minute—I bet I know who "they" are. This has Karl Rove all over it. President's poll numbers tanking? Military families making a ruckus? Public's ability to pick Howard Dean out of a Democratic lineup improving?

Kaptain Karl learned well from his mentor Lee Atwater. No need to drag out that Willie Horton ad again. First Canada's approval of gay marriage, with Massachusetts threatening, then the Supreme Court vote overturning sodomy rulings, with Tony "Supremo" Scalia warning that the whole thing could lead to gay marriage here. Not to mention that icky gay lip lock on the Oscars with the whole family watching. It's almost too easy.

Time to activate your really base? Have Pat Robertson take out a prayerful contract on straying Supremes who voted for decriminalizing gay behavior. Shortly after he issued his Operation Supreme Court Freedom Fatwa, a beam, not a log, falling at the opening of the new Constitution Museum, almost took out Sandra Day O'Swing Vote. A Rove.

Need a wedge issue? Have the Pope put out a twelve-page paper entitled, "Considerations Regarding Proposals to Give Legal Recognition to Unions Between Homosexual Persons." Homosexual persons? How quaint. All the gay Latin translators must have been let go.

I'm paraphrasing here, but the actual title was more like "Juvenilium molestorum coverupum avoidum erat." The papal posse inadvertently showed they can move at mach speed to save marriage from marauding gays, but glacial speed when it comes to saving children from molesting priests. Is a Rove.

Need a weapon of mass distraction? Have the Rev. President George Bush, answer a question about the morality of homosexuality in his press conference before his very French August vacation. "I'm mindful" which presumes a mind, "that we are all sinners." Speak for yourself, Your Militancy. I'm not cheating, lying, and war-mongering, but I am fuming. I want freedom from religion.

He compassionately conservatively quoted one of his favorite Bible passages, and cautioned people not to try to get the speck out of their neighbor's eye when they've got a log in their own. Where's my Duderonomy, Dude?

Then he called for lawyers to look into codifying the definition of marriage, one man one woman. Then he was going to look up codify. Is a Rove.

We are so being used. We are the wedgie, the butt thong between the cheeks of church and state. A Rove by any other name would still smell.

One can only hope that the Fall of Straights will be hastened by the new fall lineup.

Let me point out that gays are more visible on TV not because of some moral makeover, but because of money. Similarly, mainstream comedy clubs did not start having gay comedy nights because of their commitment to fighting homophobia, but because the comedy boom had peaked and people were getting their comedy from cable. It was about ticket prices. TV is almost passé, so it finally sees gay. We are a niche they can itch.

And I am using the royal "we" here. As I preview the fall preview, I am struck by retro lesbian invisibility. Of course, *The L-Word*—the lesbian equivalent of *Queer as Folk*—is a welcome entrant into gay carpet bombing in the culture wars. But will there be a network "Girl Meets Girl" equivalent of "Boy Meets Boy"? Why do the Fab 5's queer eyes have to help out straight guys in their pursuit of women?

As schlumpy as those guys are, they've already got the power. Why not keep it in the gay family and do *Queer Eye for the Lesbian Guy*? I know I'm attributing a lot of transformational power to the TV medium, but if the gays are mounting a doubt-based initiative to drive the fundamentalist straights crazy, then we lesbians want to be part of the fun.

(2003)

Call Me the Irreverend

You've all heard my Peggy Lee lip-syncing "Is That All There Is?" gay marriage whine. The next sound you'll hear is me jumping on the Same Sex Marriage Express. I am joining the Gay Marriage Industrial Complex!

Quite frankly, I am not going to let another gay wave pass me by. I missed the rainbow tchotchke cash cow. Who knew? I missed the gays on TV bonanza, but so did a lot of other actual gay people. I missed the Gay Cruise treasure chest. This time around, I will not be left at the altar!!

If you can't beat 'em, join 'em, and that's just what I intend to do. Judy Dlugasz, the founder of Olivia Cruises who does shipboard ceremonies—a twofer! She's brilliant— told me how to get a minister's license from the Universal Life Church.

The ULC people will e-confer your ministership at no cost

but I splurged and for $109.00, plus shipping and handling, I got the deluxe reverend package. In addition to my minister's license with my name in a very convincing liturgical font, it includes a wedding business training video for ministers, and a revised and very helpful "Ultimate Wedding & Ceremony Workbook" for the planning-impaired.

The hardbound book with sample ceremonies of weddings, funerals, and rites of passage was a bit of a disappointment. The paper is not that onion thin paper of my old Catholic missile days. It's hardbound, so it doesn't droop over my folded hands and there's no sewn-in purple placement ribbon. I might spray paint the page edges with gold.

I am most proud of my wallet-sized hologram license and the 6 × 9 inch orange laminated "Parking—Minister's Business" placard to display on my dashboard. The fine print says that parking privileges are not recognized in New York City, and that I am not authorized to do circumcisions. Otherwise I am good to go.

Like those itinerant priests who traveled during the summer months and took over for vacationing priests, but without the pedophilia, I hope to help out this summer in Provincetown.

My wedding package, The Rite Stuff, includes one hour of pre-marriage counseling, because I don't want to hear much more about it than that; the ceremony itself [I'm very good with parents]; and the reception after. My motto: "Every reception needs a wedding zinger."*

---

* I will also give a special, "Blessing of the Gay Singles" because this Mad Vow business is a bit tedious for them. I asked a single friend of mine about it and he said that sometimes he feels bad that he can't join in any rainbow games.

At first I thought my ministry would make me tax-deductible, but it turns out I have to start a church. Future plans call for "The Church of the Possible" and cashing in on all those faith-based moneys. My dream is to get Jim and Tammy's old Heritage USA Themepark at auction and start the waters flowing down the turquoise waterslide into the baptismal font once again.

And on and on I'd go. Don't call me the Right Reverend. Or even the Left Reverend. Call me the Irreverend Kate Clinton.

Until my friend from Provincetown called me and my bluff and asked me to celebrate their union of 38 years. "We'll get the justice of the peace thing but then we'd be honored to have you officiate in our living room, with a few friends. Then we'll go out to dinner."

And suddenly I am poring over my books, watching my video, worrying about my outfit and writing a special ceremony for my good friends. To celebrate their long relationship, the ups and downs and dish they've gone through together, that they lived through the AIDS plague, that they are the center of their often dysfunctional straight families, that they have to whack back their co-dependencies with large sticks, that they've both survived quadruple bypass surgeries and recoveries, that one of them still goes to T-dance, that they care for their aging surviving parents, that they've raised thousands of dollars for the Provincetown AIDS support group, that they are the most hysterical to watch the Women's NCAA basketball finals with, that every male friend of theirs has a woman's name, that they are spectacular, loyal friends and boon companions to each other. Part celebration, part roast, I am as nervous about this occasion as when I first began to perform. And honored beyond measure and surprise to be asked to celebrate my friends' love.

Get your licenses. Celebrate your friends. We'll make this marriage thing ours yet. As that old dyke Susan B. said, "Failure is impossible."

(2004)

Let's Hear It For the Boys

In today's modern world, it's so hard to stay au courant. Just ask Tom Ridge. When there was all that chatter about a terrorist group planning to interfere with the election—and they would not specify if it was the same group that had interfered with the election the last time—the feds quarantined several blocks and buildings in New York and New Jersey. Some doubted Tom and his timing, so he reluctantly revealed that the four-year-old information was discovered on floppies from an old Kaypro found on the border of Pakistan. A pastel is going to be added to the color wheel of terror indicating, "Never mind."

Apparently some new old chatter has sent the Vatican into lockdown. The bishop of Boston has been selling off the holy real estate because the church needs the money to finance the pedophilia buyouts.

In one of the buildings slated for redevelopment—right next door to a parish house—workers discovered a 30-year-old copy of *Our Bodies, Our Selves.* It was immediately translated into the Latin and carrier-pigeoned to the Vatican.

Omnium hellium brokium loosum.

The pope had a tantrum, ergo, he got his steno, head of the Congregation for the Doctrine of the Faith—the Cardinal aptly named Ratzinger—to draft a thirty-seven page paper called, "On the Collaboration of Men and Women in the Church and in the World." Or in the Latin, "Bee-otchium Slapium."

In this latest papal Post-it, His Against StemCelledness lays the blame for many modern ills—bloggers, those multipocketed pants with the zip-off lower leg, Kelly Ripa's speaking voice—squarely where it belongs. Radical feminism.

Talk about old information. Has someone at the Vatican been watching too many reruns of the "That 60s Show"?

Let's do the time warp again! A 2,000-year-old Christian identity movement still bedeviled by radical feminism? Say it is so! And where do I sign up?

The pape-istle claims that the radical feminist [and I just like saying that] view of equality has inspired ideologies which call into question the family—the two parent structure of mother and father—and seek to make homosexuality and heterosexuality virtually equivalent. In short, ix-nay on the women priests and the gay marriage.

It also declares that radical feminism [schwing!] seeks to eliminate the biological differences between man and woman. Before they start firing up the black smokestacks, I hope the Pope gets around to commissioning the paper blaming the elimination of men and women in general on radical masculinism.

Actually he may have something in the papal pipeline. When Hellboy George visited the Pope at the Vatican, the Pope did chastise him for the war in Iraq. George smiled and leaned into him and whispered, "Tell someone who cares, old man." I think he did anyway.

Then George asked His Celibacy to get the U.S. archbishops behind him against gay marriage, or as JPII likes to call it "legalization of evil." Lo, the papal rift was mended. From then on, their communion was divine.

And don't tell me W. wasn't paying attention at the old seat of the Inquisition. Under Bush II's reign, the wall between church and state has pretty well been taken down. Think of it as a productivity thing: at the rate the church-state merger is going, soon there will be a dual use confessional/ballot box. Think of the time savings.

"Bless me father for I have sinned: I support stem cell research, I keyed a Lexus SUV in the parking lot, and I am going to vote for John Kerry."

"My child, for your penance you are going to have to watch *The Passion of the Christ* fifteen times, and for keying my Lexus, you are going to have to blow me right now."

(2004)

Darling,
We're Still Divine

FRIDAY, TWO WEEKS BEFORE THE election, I was in the Atlanta airport, boarding a flight to Salt Lake City to perform at the National PFLAG Conference. Hint: The Cheneys were not scheduled to appear. In fact, on a scale of one to PFLAG, the Cheneys are, to quote the Vice Cusser, "Go f**k yourself."

I was sporting my "John Kerry: A Stronger America" button even though it had been deconstructed by the Swift Boat Font-Makers for Truth as clearly weak on defense. The plane was being boarded by zones and I was beginning to think they were putting Kerry supporters in the ozone of steerage, when a couple came up to me, eyed my button and without a hello, how are you, intoned, "A vote for John Kerry will hasten the Second Coming."

For a moment I thought they were dissing the new boarding system—first class, second coming, etc. I said, "Excuse me?" They smiled and repeated their mantra slower and louder as if I did not speak their language.

In a moment I now believe was divinely inspired, I smiled and replied, "Does that mean you will be leaving soon?"

We all have our belief systems. I believe there was voter fraud. I also believe that anti-gay marriage initiatives, which we did not put on swing state ballots, were used to get out the vote. We were so used. We were the wedgie, the butt thong between the cheek of church and the cheek of state. That's the bad news. Supposedly four million Christian fundamentalists pulled the lever for W stands for War. So much for reversing the curse. In those damnable exit polls, they whined that liberals had made them feel guilty about their faith. They were not values voters, but victim voters. That a 35-year-old gay identity movement can threaten a 2005-year-old Christian identity movement is, I believe, the good news.

Besides the obvious protest strategies of not paying taxes, suing to tax churches, refusing to sit on juries, refusing to serve in the military, caterwauling at family weddings, starting impeachment proceedings for an illegal war, snapping down your yoga mat five times a day wherever you are and loudly davening for democracy, or driving the wrong way down one-way streets dragging Terry Macauliffe face down for a couple blocks, I've got an idea. No, I'm not moving out of the country. I already live in the tiny island nation of New York City. Nor am I going on some four-year gay cruise setting sail down the Potomac on January 19th, 2005.

Since we are in the midst of a religious war, tricked out as a cultural war, I want to do a religious reality show called "The Spirit is Willing," a weekly show on religion and sexuality. The GLBT community is a deeply spiritual community. After all, it takes quite a leap of faith to come out. Faith in ourselves, faith in others, in individual freedom, in divine justice. The set would have the familiar Christian broadcast look—gray industrially carpeted stairs, large potted palms, and lucite pulpits. But the message is completely different—Gay is Go-d, Om is Homo, the Golden Lamé Rule.

We'd draw from our rich tradition of gay spiritual leaders, sing those old-time gay spirituals, feature a religion of the week—Islam, Buddhism, Wicca, Catholicism—and their position on gays and gays in that religion. The show would have weekly features: a panel going soul-to-soul to counter textural antigay teachings; five minutes of world religion news—"The Pope Watch", "You Say Moolah, I say Mullah", "The Gism Schism"; each week long snaking lines of people coming forward to witness and be welcomed and blessed as they come out—a little pop on the forehead and they fall backward in the welcoming arms of other gay people.

I have pitched this idea to both LOGO, and Here! I dare them or any other of the triune networks to produce it.

It's time for a Second Coming Out of gay people.

(2004)

SURRENDER, LAURAS

Besides war, women, and the war on women, W stands for Wayback machine. We are on that slipperiest slope to the pre-est feminism. First Lady catfights about cookie baking. Surrender Circles where women pledge to abandon the myth of equality and submit to their husbands. Women as torturers, serial killers, and corrupt corporate players too. "'She's had work done," instead of "She's working." Adoring wives of Promise Creepers. Stepford Wives re-tooled as Desperate (for what?) Housewives. Suburban Soccer Moms in ungainly mini-vans, now Security Moms in momogrammed, armored-up humvees. Men with Viagra, women without hormones. Watch out. An African-American Woman is Secretary of State and I know I should be happier. Women have bell curves and are said to be innately deficient in science and math. Arm every woman! Kidding. But there would be gun control in no time.

GETTING STEAMED

THE ANNOYING EL NIÑOISTAS DANCED a brisk "We told you so" to an Apocalypso beat the day forty-eight inches of snow fell on Denver. The magnitude of the storm was not measured in inches per hour but by the fact that—gasp!—the Broncos couldn't fly out of the airport. Personally, I think it was Mother Nature's farewell tribute to John Denver.

The air over New York City has been overheated for months. Wall Street is in the eye of the storm with more high pressure and precipitous drops than the Weather Channel in a hurricane. Chief meteorologist Alan Greenspan, with pointers and clickers, explains global market warming, working backward in front of a blank blue wall. I felt like that annoying von Trapp kid after Julie

Andrews teaches him "Do, a deer, a female deer," and he whines, "But tit doesn't mean anything."

Speaking of hot air, President Clinton, voiceless from partying all night with his fiftieth-birthday bride, barely broke a sweat on global warming. I can't look at the guy anymore. Not since I mistakenly clicked onto an MSNBC special on the distinguishing features of the Presidential peepee. Don't show me the monty.

The El Niñoistas also attribute the unseasonably balmy Northeast fall to the warm waters off Mexico. I don't. I think the heat wave was caused by the huge amounts of hot air spewing from the national mall when the Promise Creepers stood in their GAP shirts for the Million White Man Mingle. Patricia Ireland, the president of NOW, one of the few women to rain on the nonparade, was burned at the stake, which also fanned the Fahrenheit a few degrees.

That day C-SPAN was part of my required viewing, and unfortunately, C-SPAN insisted on protecting its G-rating and did not follow the Lesbian Avengers when they marched bare-chested through the throngs.

Most of the reviews written by women were basically puff pieces: You know, we disagree with the things they stand for, but they seemed like nice enough guys. Even the intrepid *Village Voice* writer Donna Minkowitz, who went undercover, said she had a nice time and seemed more excited about passing as a guy than what passed as compassion. These reviews sounded like the neighbors' description of the homicidal maniac next door: He was quiet, worked hard, loved his family. I got steamed.

My temperature rose again leafing through *Life* magazine's

100 movers and shakers of the millennium and found there was not one woman listed. *Vanity Fair*'s special issue on the sixty-five most powerful Americans had two women—*The Washington Post*'s Katharine Graham and Secretary of State Madeleine Albright. Unlike the men who were photographed alone, Graham and Albright appeared with their staffs, apparently unable to handle the photo-shoot by themselves.

I'm not the only one adding a little estrogen-laced steam to the atmosphere. Janet Reno is steamed. And I don't blame her. Seems some of the White House tapes were mislabeled. There was a tape of Chelsea's sixteenth birthday party. A couple of tapes of Ted and Jane sleeping in the Lincoln Bedroom. You know they are taping those. Newt's got a little peephole and late at night you can hear him urging, "Come on, baby, show Newtie your contract." Somehow there was also Al Gore's tape of Ellen's coming-out episode, which Dan Quayle likes to play backward and show Ellen going back into her closet.

(1997)

Hello, Dolly!

ON THE CUSP OF WOMEN'S History Month, the papers announced that an embryologist from Scotland had for the first time successfully cloned a sheep whose fleece was white as snow and named it Dolly. When asked for comment on the implications of such a discovery, the fabulously named Dr. Ursula Goodenough, a cell biologist at Washington University in St. Louis, quipped, "There'll be no need for men."

Hello, Dolly!

Before examining less promising implications, let's have a look at the great Scot and what he did. Dr. Ian Wilmut, a father of three children whose names he has trouble remembering, is described most eagle-scoutishly by his colleagues as "careful, diligent, honest, and thoughtful." That's supposed to make us all feel better, but somehow it doesn't quite allay the worries. Plus, he wears sheep cologne.

The day after the announcement and faster than you can say "how to make a knapsack bomb," the instructions for cloning were on the Internet at www.anewewe.org. I downloaded them and despite that "do not try this at home" warning, I did.

The recipe is quite simple: First, take a cell from a sheep and keep it in a tissue while removing the DNA-containing nucleus from an unfertilized sheep's egg. So far, so good. Next, fuse them together into an embryo.

As in every family recipe, Dr. Wilmut left some instruction or ingredient out. Try as I might, I could not get them to fuse, even though I played *Peter and the Wolf* very softly in a darkened room. Might have been the wrong voltage. I was, therefore, unable to transfer the embryo into a surrogate mother sheep, as Dr. Wilmut had done, where it was supposed to divide and develop like a normal embryo. It's probably just as well. My apartment is tiny, and there are rules about pets.

The implications of this new development are enormous:

- Miss Shari Lewis won't have to buy new tube socks.
- "Babe" will clone sequels.
- Nursery rhymes will have to be updated (e.g., Mary had a little lamb, little lamb, little lamb, Mary had a little lamb all by herself").
- Children's songs will have to be updated (e.g., "Old MacDonald had a farm . . . and on his farm he had . . . a pigsheep—with an 'oink bah' here and a 'oink bah' there, here an 'oink', there an 'bah', everywhere an 'oink bah'").

- Pope John Paul, who himself was cloned from a large kielbasa, orders a revision of that "Lamb of God" song.
- *My Daughter, Myself* will become a bestseller from the Boston Women's Health Book Collective.

Meanwhile, Woolite workers are doing overtime. Insomniacs are thrilled. Polar Fleece people are panicked. Condom makers ecstatic. Narcissists vindicated. Term limits obsolete.

Unlike Dr. Morethan Goodenough, my first thought was not the end of husbandry but, "Oh great, just what we need—more sheep."

Flocks of sheep are backing off campaign-finance reform.

Democratic sheep are letting Alexis Herman take the fall for Clinton's fundraising abuses. One Republican sheep almost left town to become president of Pepperdine. In D.C., wolves in sheep's clothing are letting that town go back to grass.

(1997)

Fort Brag

Attention Bill Nye, Science Guy—galactic update! Scientists have discovered that there is a North-South axis in the galaxy, but they are reluctant to say which end is up. Me, too. They have also discovered a monster fountain of antimatter erupting outward from the core of the Milky Way. The find, which came to them one morning at a Denny's Grand Slam breakfast, has made them alter their neat image of a disk-shaped galaxy to one of a fried egg with steam shooting out of the yolk. In laymen's terms, it's become harder to keep your sunny side up.

I can see why. Saying he wants to devote himself full time to getting Christians elected to public office, that blue-eyed uber-Christian egghead, Ralph Reed, has left his job as head of the Christian Coalition. As if up to this point he's been spending his time just trying to perfect a tuna

casserole for the church potluck, now he says he's going to
get busy, and I for one am nervous.

Nervous, too, especially after I read the findings of Anna
Simmons, assistant professor of anthropology at UCLA.
She is the author of a new book, *The Company They Keep: Life
Inside U.S. Army Special Forces.* In a column in *The New York Times,*
she summarized some of the things she discovered during
the year and a half she observed elite twelve-man A-teams
in the Marines.

The title of her column was, "In War Let Men Be Men."
My java had not yet bridged some early synapses, so I
mistakenly expected irony. It was early; I was groggy.

According to Professor Simmons, the post–Cold War
era might seem like a perfect time for women to be in
combat units. She says, and apparently believes, that we are
not engaged in any conflicts in the world, and that peace-
keeping is our main mission. Nonetheless, she claims that
women in combat actually endanger our troops. Why?
Because G.I. Janes inhibit male bonding. It is this
bonding, she says, that enables men to survive the stress of
working closely under difficult conditions of cramped
space, long hours, hardship, and extreme danger.

At this point, the java's jumping and the content is high,
so I'm tracking her argument. As she leads up to revealing
the secret sources of male bonding, I'm expecting her to say
something like "counting pushups with each other," or
"shouting encouraging things to each other," but no, she
concludes that the way to build trust lies in bragging about
sexual conquests!

What's up with that?

Simmons says simply that G.I. Gals make the G.I. Guys self-conscious about claiming to be all that they can be. The presence of women makes men clam up about their reputed prowess or hup to the task of backing up their boasting. That interferes with the bonding process and thus destroys critical unit cohesiveness and combat readiness.

Admittedly, I was not having a Phi Beta Cappuccino, but I thought I missed something in Professor Simmons's column. I looked back. Did she say her degree was in Anthro-apology?

Ask yourself, if men had not exaggerated their sexual conquests, would we have lost the Civil, the Big, the Great, and the War to End All? Was that what happened in Vietnam?

From what I've seen in Aberdeen and other military trials, I'd have to conclude that it's time to get men out of the military. In war, let women be men; in peace, let men be women.

(1997)

VIAGRA FALLS

I'M NO MARGARET MEAD (ALTHOUGH one Halloween
I cut in some blunt bangs, slipped on a sarong and some
sensible shoes, and carried a big walking stick), but I would
have to say that straight people are in the middle of a bigger
end-of-the-century sex panic than gay people could ever
dream of having. On a scale of 1 to Jeff Stryker, it's big.

Who pushed the actual panic button is debatable. Ken
Starr—always in that driveway, always with that Big Gulp-
size Styrofoam cup of coffee, relentlessly playing "Six
Degrees of Monica Lewinsky"—gave rise to President
Clinton's Unwilling National Dialogue on Sex. Every press
conference is turned into a town meeting on sex, no matter
what visiting head of state is standing next to the First Babe
Magnet. "Are you an insatiable sex addict?" "Do you consider oral sex, sex?" (I am so glad he's not into anal sex.)

Even the grande dame of press conferences, Helen Thomas, shouts out, "Mr. President! Show me the monty!" One suspects there is someone behind the podium and that's why he talks so long.

With banks merging with banks merging with insurance companies merging with entertainment conglomerates merging with phone companies merging with networks merging with arms makers and with nations merging into one European Union, we are—wink wink, nudge nudge—told that bigger is better. Better for whom? Certainly not for poor people, who are actually described as the "unbanked." Not better for me. I dialed a wrong number the other day and bought a small prison by mistake.

Into this straight sex panic comes the panacea, the so-called magic bullet, Pfizer's Riser, the Mo' Bigger Blues, Viagra. What was originally tested as angina treatment to help blood flow to the heart proved unsuccessful in opening the coronary arteries but very successful in keeping a penis erect. This side effect was discovered when test subjects were reluctant to turn in their leftover pills. The drug's name, suggesting vigor and a trip to Niagara Falls, had been kicking around the company for years. So had *Sunny Boner,* but *Viagra* seemed a better fit.

Fueled by stories from Rogained newscasters smirking over their noticeably rising anchor desks, an average of 10,000 prescriptions were written per day in the first month of availability. Some enterprising doctors had rubber stamps made to prevent hand cramping, while other unscrupulous doctors sold through www.penispill.com without so much as a hello, how are you, first I'm going to take your blood pressure. Who knew there was so much impotence in this, the last remaining superpower?

And Viagra is not just for diabetic geezer boomers in Florida, which already looks thicker and straighter on my map. I asked my harried-looking local pharmacist if any women were taking it. She was standing in front of a hastily written THE VIAGRA IS HERE! sign. She shook her head and said with a glimmer of disgust on her usually stoic face, "No, only old men with canes."

What is the trickle-down effect, if you'll pardon the image, for the gay community? My gay men friends think it will make straight men happier, which is good for gay men who are often the target of straight sexual resentment. Maybe with something to do at home other than spin cats by the tail, Jesse Helms, Strom Thurmond, even Dan Burton will retire.

It promises to be one heck of a summer. Viagra is already a registered drag name in Miami. Tea dances will be sponsored by Absolut Viagra and replaced by hour-long V dances. Don't Panic! will put out a BUGGER IS BETTER T-shirt. At circuit parties, renamed Eli Lillith Fairs, someone will have to announce, "Don't eat the brown Viagra." There will be Viagra testing at the Gay Games in Amsterdam. If you're not on it, you're disqualified.

In all the Viagra-rama there is never any mention of Viagra vérité: safe sex, condoms, responsibility, or, dare I say it, rape. I for one am nervous. I am going to stay home this summer and watch the WNBA. In that alternating week that I am gay, I'll watch that missing episode of *Ellen*—"Did Somebody Say Cochlea?"—in which Ellen goes in for a routine hearing test and is set upon by a right-wing ear, nose, and throat man determined to enlarge her ear bone. Or maybe I'll develop something for gals. Here's a name that's been knocking around for years—Virago.

(1998)

SURRENDER, LAURAS

LATELY I FEEL AS IF I am living in a John Grisham novel: *The Chad.*

Here's the Grishamic vignette: A bunch of old CIA/oil guys, all jacked up on Viagra, get together at their club and over cognac and Cuban cigars make a bet that they can take over the government. You know the hijinx that ensue. Absentee ballots treated like letters to Santa. Stacked court. Fox "News." On second thought, change the Viagra to Britney Spears.

The B-story line of *The Chad* is pure *Stepford Wives,* that early 1970s Ira Levin classic and major motion picture. In it, a wife new to Stepford starts a consciousness-raising group because she is appalled that all the women in her town wear flowery print dresses and seem satisfied with their domestic servitude. She uncovers the nefarious deeds of the Stepford Men's Club, which clandestinely replaces the town's wives with domestic sex robots. Actually in the B-line of this kinder sorter kinder gentler year 2001, the Stepford wife is the Surrendered Wife.

In her best-selling book, *The Surrendered Wife: A Practical Guide to Finding Intimacy, Passion, Peace with Your Man*, author and noncredentialed suggester Laura Doyle describes how she almost lost her relationship with her husband because she was constantly nagging him. When she gave up her nit-picking ways, things changed and she is now finally in the relationship she always dreamed about.

In her book and in the women's "Surrender Circles" which have sprung up as spontaneously as Promisekeeper stadium rallies, this non-Dr. Laura suggests that a woman's tasks are to take care of herself first, to overcome her desire to have more power and to abandon the myth of equality. You'll have to yank my copy of *Ms.* magazine from my cold dead hands, but I say that the second and third cancel out the first assignment.

On a long car trip, I heard Laura Doyle, self-identified "feminist and former shrew," interviewed on several radio call-in shows, and in a very warm, winning voice, from her own experience and from women she had interviewed, she opined that women have to stop controlling, criti-cizing, and interrupting their husbands. She believes women have to apologize for being disrespectful. They have to be ready to say, "Whatever you think. . . ." And, and this is the one all the radio guys loved—women must never refuse sex with their husbands, even if they're not in the mood. No Laurabot she.

The D.C. [Damn Coup] Bush women all seem to be playing their surrendered wife roles very well. New Jersey's former profiler, pro-lifer governor Christine Todd Whitman was forced to eat her pro-enviro words and swallow her water neat, with acceptable arsenic levels. Whatever you think. Condi Rice's solution to global warming is a cold war. Whatever, Rummy. And I must have missed a Page Six *Post* gossip item when I was ducking falling Mir chunks, but did Maureen Dowd get drunk at a party, come on to Hillary Clinton, and get rebuffed, and so has to do every other *New York Times* column-hating Hillary, that most unsurrendered of wives?

There's a Laura theme happening in the country. Dr. Laura Schlessinger, the radio/TV talk show host just had to surrender her show. I for one will miss her. No one else has kept gay issues so effectively in the news lately. Bush II is like living in one of those Ex-gay ads. If she ever says, "Whatever you think," the "you idiot" is understood.

And have you noticed that Laura Bush, "the anti-Hillary" to John Podhoretz or "First" as that rollicking Nicknamer-in-Chief has cleverly dubbed her, is among the disappeared? Or did she just run off with Ralph Nader?

It happened shortly after Laura Bush's underreported remarks in favor of a woman's right to abortion. She seems to spend a lot of time in Texas, keeping tabs on the wild blonde twin at the University of Texas and putting the finishing touches on their dream Texas getaway [from what?], which is described as sprawling, lowslung ranch with door frames flush with their beloved scrubland. It sounds as if it were designed along the magisterial lines of a corrugated U-Stor-It facility.

A *Washington Post* story described Laura Bush as seeing every-thing in its place including herself. One long-time woman friend admiringly shared that Laura likes to relax by taking books off shelves and Cloroxing the cabinets. Why isn't that weirder than not baking cookies? Whatever you say.

The Stepford Men's Club was a heavily guarded old manor house with a strictly enforced dress code. W. has insisted on the reinstatement of a dress code in the White House. No denim. No shirt, no tie, no service. Pants with creases. No thongs, but lots of wink wink, nudge nudge thong jokes.

And though very little mention has been made of it, no pantsuits for women. Federal workers shopping at your finer women's stores in Chevy Chase have been heard to inquire, "What color does that burka come in?" "Do you have that chador in linen?" "Can I get the carpal tunnel wrist brace monogrammed?"

(2001)

ALL THE PRESIDENT'S WOMEN

EVERY GAL NEEDS A HOBBY. In light of recent events—and really, there was so little light—and in keeping with my New Year's Resolution, (not the one involving Helen Mirren), I decided to neglect my massive heartache about my country [did I mention I love my country?] I decided to take up the Bush Women.

This administration loves the little women, so there are many, many, many, many from whom to chose. But with W's [stands for war] approval ratings at 117% according to Arthur Anderson, I figured I better leave Laura alone and look to the next line of offense, the Matalin/Hughes/Rice troika.

During Tom Brokaw's very special "Touched by a President" reality-TV prequel to *The West Wing*, the threesome's incredible power became clear. They're right down the hall from him!

Mary Matalin, aide-du-camp to Dick Cheney, always looks as if she has just returned from some midday oral surgery and the novocaine in her lower lip hasn't worn off.

Mr. Karen Hughes who keeps the Dub on time and on message frankly scares me more than Kate O'Beirne.

So I settled on Condoleezza Rice and found lots of dish in an interview in Oprah's *O* magazine. It was in *O*'s "Freedom" issue just before "The Sap of Luxury" a great article about maple syrup. In her introduction, Oprah opines, "In all my years of interviewing, I have never been prouder to spell my name w-o-m-a-n than after spending time with Condoleeza Rice." *O* is apparently a spellcheck-free space.

They talked about how cool it is to have an unusual name. Condi's first name is derived from an Italian musical term meaning "to play with sweetness," and her last name is great cold with balsamic vinegar for an afternoon snack or just to take the edge off hunger. Condi's passions are shopping, exercise, classical music, and Joseph Stalin.

But then along came Enron, and sadly, I have lapsed in pursuit of my resolution though not of Helen Mirren. When one is trying to keep up with the many strands of the Enron story, one does the Condi-minimum.

And there are more strands to this story than there are fiber optics in Global Crossing.

Oops, sorry, they just tanked.

There's the heartache of the Lay family left with nothing, nothing. W's mother-in-law losing eight thousand dollars. Turns out, she really didn't. Recusements. Dick Cheney stonewalling on his energy panel's right to privacy all the way to a decision by the Supreme Court. Odds are 5 to 4 for the Veep. I'm waiting for him to announce that there will be no future elections because they are just too divisive for homeland security.

The Karl Rove–Ralph Reed connection. The bona fide suicide of an Enron employee who was about to talk. No strands to Hillary Clinton and Vince Foster, yet. Ari Fleischer spinning more than an Olympic skater on steroids. The we-did-nothing-wrong stance of the White House. And they might not have. Which is scarier?

If nothing sticks to the White House, it should prove once and for all that there is no liberal media.

My favorite strands involve the pseudo-égalité that Enron women have achieved. They are no mere sexual objects, but players. Sherron S. Watkins, an Enron exec, warned Kenny Boy of company implosions. Maureen Castaneda had taken some of the shreds home to use as packing material and noticed some cute but questionable names. Nancy Temple of Arthur Anderson wrote a memo that fired up their shredders.

These women are described as "high enough on the corporate ladder to drive the action," "close enough to the corridors of power to hear secrets" and "technically proficient enough to figure out what is going on." I've got a little tear in my eye.

(2002)

Extreme Makeover

AT KIOSKS AND BUS STOPS all over New York, there are posters for the movie *Resident Evil: Apocalypse*. And almost on every poster, someone has graffitied a very tasteful P at the beginning of the first word. That about sums up the election for me.

But not quite. The final summation comes on the reverse side of the President Evil billboard, with a poster for the ABC series Desperate Housewives. The series' tagline is "Everyone has a little dirty laundry."

Now I know Michael Moore has told me not to be a Downer Dem, so flattened by the Juggernaut of George that I am not able to walk upright, but when I saw the poll that Democratic Soccer Moms had been switching to become Republican Security Moms because they believe that the resident of the White House will best protect them from terrorism, I did have a moment.

In *New York* magazine, Naomi Wolf, whose alpha plan for the Gore man the Republicans gleefully derided four years ago, credits the original girlieman, Karen Hughes, with the extreme makeover. And all without giving each and every housewife a new Pontiac!

In her "The Sexes" column, Wolf writes that Hughes has managed the transformation first by bringing out the warm, fuzzy side of the Vice Cusser through the tender stories from his blushing bride. And second by having Aura Bush humanize her hell-is-on-the-way husband with purred stories of him wrastling with issues of war and peace. Which cause him to fall off his bike a lot.

And though it pained Wolf to say it, she said it nonetheless: The Republicanizing of the desperate housewives is all Teresa Heinz Kerry's fault. For by keeping her Heinz name, she is "publicly, subliminally cuckolding Kerry with the power of another man—a dead Republican, at that." Hold the mustard! He might as well change his name to Harry Kerry.

W stands for War on Women. The Administration's policy on women is often hard to see because it is written in the font size of pharmaceutical ads. So let me enlarge it a little: The heading is that wives must be subordinate to their husbands. And here is the fine print:

- propose a constitutional ban on abortion
- pledge to support only antichoice judges
- enforce a law banning abortion without any exception for the woman's health
- maintain a law blocking abortion for poor, young, and military women

- submit a Human Life Amendment conferring personhood on the fertilized egg
- fund abstinence-only sex education
- extend the global gag rule on contraceptive education worldwide.

Meanwhile, Bush gets away with all this by "feminizing" some of his rhetoric, especially in his acceptance speech at the Republican Convention, where Hughes's handiwork was obvious. "Two-thirds of all moms also work outside the home," Bush said, "and government must take your side."

His government? Where's he been for four years? He hasn't exactly been hiking the minimum wage or funding free quality child care. Nor is he proposing it.

But the rhetoric is the thing. And Hughes made sure he talked emotionally about the wounded soldiers and the kids who just wanted their mothers and fathers back. Message: "A good man with a big heart," as Laura put it.

And a weird mind. A few days after the convention, Bush was speaking to a crowd and was denouncing medical malpractice suits when he let this one slip: "Too many OBGYNs aren't able to practice their love with women all across this country."

Am I the only one who found that creepy?

(2004)

SUMMER'S RATIONALE

WHOOPEE! GALS, DO NOT WORRY if you get an IRS audit! Just plead "The Summer's Rationale"—no, not sunstroke—that women are innately inferior to men in math and science. Larry Summers, the president of Harvard said it; therefore it must be true. We are so off the hook!

No wonder, what with all that math, that my pretty little head can't make one whit of sense out of all the jabbering about the imminent destruction of social security. Even if the Treasury Secretary Snow showed the little white vials again I don't think it adds up. No matter. If I'm hearing the president right, the only number I have to worry about is fifty-five. Since I'm just over that age, seems you young uns, you genderqueer, transmen and women, trannyfags, trannydykes and bois are going to have to pick up the tab for me.

The theatre tickets, the dry-cleaning, the lunches. No, here, I'll get the tip. Does anyone have change for this queer as a five dollar bill? The descendants of old Kinsey have discovered the dirt on not quite honest Abe, in their "All the Presidents are Gay Men Manhattan Project." Upcoming bombshells: Teddy Roosevelt—A Bear!; Howard Taft—Big Bottom; Woodrow "Woody" Wilson—Circuit Party Boy.

With my lucky number 55, I feel like I have won lottery! I might privatize, I mean take up ownership of all my money and move into any of the planned so-called Gray Havens— Encore in Los Angeles, Rainbow Vision in Santa Fe or Casa de Gay Manana in Puerto Villarta. Despite the generous support of the youths, we gay geezer boomers are going to need all the non-profit low income housing we can get. Of course, if those evangelicals would ever get helpful and step off into the rapture, and if they would just hand us the keys to their places during lift-off, our housing shortages could be over. You do the aftermath! Gay Realtors for the Rapture! Then, of course, queer eye makeovers for all those darling little split-level ranches.

And not that I need those pesky science skills I don't have anyway. Abortion causes cancer. AIDS is spread by spit. Evolution is devolution. To look at those dear dueling banjo Bush twins, scowling into the sun behind Curious George at the inauguration or at that other royal offspring with the swastika armband, is to hypothesize that perhaps there has been a survival of the shallowest. The president actually said that the jury is still out on evolution and seems to believe that the Scopes Trial is a blind test for mouthwash. The creationists don't say the world was made by god, they say it was created by wink wink, nudge nudge, "Intelligent Design" which sounds like some Conran catalogue or an obit for that big queen Philip Johnson.

In junior and senior high schools throughout the empire, straight teens, emboldened by federally scanctioned homophobia, are now beaning gay teens with science books covered with the traditional hand drawn hearts encircling the words, "SueAnn loves JimBob in a platonic way and pledges to abstain from sex until marriage," next to school board decals that disclaim "Evolution is just a theory." Don't save your filibuster for later. What will they go after next, gravity? As we gray gays used to say, "There's no such thing as gravity; the earth sucks."

Actually save Buster. In her first days on the job, Secretary of Education, Margaret Spellings instead of denouncing the $240,000 her department paid to "independent journalist" Armstrong Williams, boldly went after the cartoon bunny Buster, who has asthma and is the child of divorced bunnies. Hasn't he suffered enough? Leave no child of divorced bunnies behind. Spellings said the explicit video post card Arthur sent from Vermont at sugaring time of kids with two lesbian moms promoted the dreaded "tolerance and diversity."

For James Dobson of Fuckus on the Family, tolerance and diversity are code words for homosexual agenda. His overheated gaydar machine had just exposed the treachery of SpongeBob Squarepants who likes to hold hands with his friend Patrick and watch their favorite video of Mermaid Man and Barnacle Boy. In addition to skipping the evolution unit, apparently they are no longer teaching that unit on genus/species differentiation between homo sapiens and homo cartoonum either.

Who needs science when begats and bigots will do? I do need a hit of whatever Laura "Passport to Manhood" Bush is having.

(2005)

My Malformative Years

. . .

The political is so personal. Actual people are so inconvenient when a hardening of the categories meets dear flesh and blood. Of the friends we see uncomfortably after we've come out to them. Or don't see again. Of new friends. Of the small children who sense something is wrong, but still want to go screaming through the car wash with their aunt. Political meets personal during family dinner table conversation when the decision is made not to go there. Or to go there. The energy of trying to be in the closet can erase one's childhood memories. Coming out as a lesbian is good practice for coming out of the peace closet. My dear old Dad, my personal patriarch and in-house libertarian, unconditionally affirmed the dialectic. We are here. We are queer. It takes some getting used to, people. Don't just talk among yourselves.

Almost Out of Come-Outs

You'll be happy to know that October 11 was the Eleventh Annual National Coming Out Day.

As a proudly observant lesbian, I participated once again. I'm getting to be a pro at this.

On the very first Coming Out Day, I learned never to come out to a close relative in a moving vehicle.

I am now out to all of my relatives. My ten-month-old grandniece seemed a bit bewildered but supportive in a goo-goo-ga-ga sort of way.

In a very misguided third year, I learned the critical preposition/proposition difference between coming out to and coming on to. Space restrictions preclude the juicy details, but you can find them on my website: www.ingout.com.

During my ninth observance of National Coming Out

Day, I discovered that coming out can be helpful in vacating the neighboring seat even on a crowded flight.

After eleven years of coming out, I am, quite frankly, almost out of come-outs. It's become quite the challenge. I've considered ringing neighbors' doorbells while wearing some drag king outfit, shrilling fabulously, "I'm a lesbian!" into their bemused faces, and opening my Tinky Winky pocketbook for treats.

I've also taken to announcing to my friends and family the number of shopping days until next National Coming Out Day and gently notifying them where I am registered for gifts.

This October 11, Abe Lincoln came out. Some historians, along with the playwright Larry Kramer, have pressed the claim that the tall, dreamy, raw-boned President was gay. This was based on the discovery of love letters from Joshua Speed, a longtime companion of the Great Emancipator. DNA tests were also done on sheets from the Lincoln bedroom and revealed unusually high thread counts. The Log Cabin Republicans have become even more insufferable.

I learned early on from my coming out experiences with my eldest brother that repetition is a good thing. Each year I would come out to him. We wouldn't talk about it again until the next National Coming Out Day, when he would say, "Is that all you ever talk about?" Repeatedly coming out to him did not inflate my totals, but it was good practice.

Recently, at his son's wedding reception, my brother insisted that my partner of twelve years and I get onto the dance floor for couples. He was proud when we outlasted many of the others.

But for some, every day is National Go Back In Day.

George W is against adoption by gay couples, anti-discrimination laws, same-sex marriage, and employment nondiscrimination, though he says gays can participate equally where the death penalty is concerned.

Gary Bauer doesn't believe a healthy society can encourage homosexuality.

Pat Buchanan believes homosexuals are hell-bent on Satanism and suicide.

Dr. Laura thinks the whole thing is disgusting and feels victimized when she says so.

I used to think that the virulence of such opposition to anything gay was in direct proportion to the growing strength of the gay movement. But we are not that strong. I have come to realize that it is the end stage of heterosexuality. But all is not virulence.

This year, President Clinton proclaimed June "Gay Pride Month." Amazing what a lame duck President can do.

Bill Bradley has taken a stand for including gays and lesbians as a protected group under the Civil Rights Act of 1964.

And the Registry of Historic Landmarks has now recognized the Stonewall Inn, site of the beginning of the modern gay liberation movement.

So Trent Lott can compare homosexuality to alcoholism and kleptomania all he wants. Gay people have learned to take insults as invitations and warnings as welcomes.

We plan to get drunk on gay power and steal ourselves an election.

(1999)

Alternative Family Week

FOR MY DIAMOND JUBILEE LESBIAN Years, I had envisioned Mother Earth Watch trips with my fellow crones, counting hawks in migration over Lesbos; circling up the silver Airstreams and swapping coming out stories around the camp fire after a day of convoying in voter registration drives throughout the South; or popping out my uppers and gumming the pretty young things who attended to my every need at Amazon Manor. No wait, that last one was a movie I rented.

But at the rate my friends are having kids, my late lesbo a go golden years are going to be more about attending bat mitzvahs, chaperoning proms, attending college graduations, and cheering at Olympic Gymnastic Events.

Go figure.

After twenty-five years of the right's steady drum beat thumping family values, the left's challenge to gender roles and the medical middle's advances in reproductive science, lesbians and now gay men are having and getting kids. Lots of them. Many of them are now having second kids. Apparently rollicking barebackers are not the only ones forgoing protection.

Provincetown's Third Annual Alternative Family Week last July was like a promenade at the Breeder's Cup, with serious stroller gridlock throughout town, many of them double-wides. The A&P ran out of Huggies. There were networking groups for gay parents, play groups for kids and more face painting than the Saturday night drag shows. For the first time since the heyday of the mid-eighties full service lesbian music scene, we offered childcare during my show. After years of maturing as a movement, self-hate seems to have decreased as evidenced in the paraphrase, "I'm having my baby, what a wonderful way of saying how much I love me."

In the beginning of the Gay Baby Boom, I thought of forming a group called ACWC, "Adult Children Without Children." It seemed like we shouldn't be having baby showers with Michelin tire party favors, but going away parties. Friends trying to get pregnant were semi-present in wild two-week mood swings. Dinner conversations involved debates about fresh sperm versus frozen sperm. That was just appetizers. Those friends adopting kids were stunned by alternating bouts of anticipation then disappointment, and some literally left the country for months at a time to get their children. Some put their new children on credit cards. No judgment here; I just don't think one should name the child Optima.

With the arrival of the babies, friends were absent due to horrific sleep deprivation, worry, and the sheer goo-goo-ga-ga magic of single or couple parenting. Full sentences, late nights out [later than 8:00 P.M.] and conspiratorial eye-rolling during interminable volunteer meetings were things of the past. I had my abandonment issues.

If I weren't such a sucker for babies and kids, I would have organized ACWC chapters statewide. I like kids so much, I don't have them. After about two hours with kids, I have a tendency to glaze over and after a babysitting scare involving Lincoln logs and a butane lighter, I thought it wouldn't be right. So I don't have kids. That I know of. There was that softball summer. But the point is no one has gotten in touch with me.

Like a priest doing marriage counseling, I do have some advice. I was a child once, I helped raise two younger sibs, I have nine fabulous nieces and nephews, and at last count fourteen small ones with friends. The New York twins are due in September. I am not uncredentialed.

When I ask my friends if they are going to raise their kids to be gay, they have a moment of semi-horror and say, "Oh, no, I am going to let her make her own choice." Listen, we live in a heterosexual mall, I say if we really are going to try this experiment, let's give the kids some help, and get some gold lamé on those little boys and a nice little tool belt on those girls.

Most of my friends feel the pressure to prove that gay people can be great parents and raise spectacular kids or they have read that study that said every single moment is a teachable moment for their kids. Everybody could use a nap. That's where people like me come in. Kids love to see me coming, because compared to most of the three-year-olds they know, I am a major slacker. My idea of an educational field trip is to pop them in the car and drive through the car wash screaming.

Too many of my friends are choosing private schools over public schools when their kids are school age. This saddens me because as a former high school English teacher, I would have loved to have seen some gay parents stroll into my room on parent–teacher night. I look forward to gay parents changing the heterosexist culture of public schools, soccer leagues, and Scouts as they roll on through their kids development.

One way or the other, we are changing the structure of family. It's about time. The school shootings in Littleton, Colorado show again that the vaunted nuclear family at its whitest, upper class best is not working. It's time for the Village people to raise some children.

(1999)

MY MALFORMATIVE YEARS

THAT DETECTOR YOU HAVE TO pass through as you enter a video store actually does two things, neither of which has anything to do with preventing purloined copies of Kevin Costner's *The Postman* from tripping the alarm. First, it destroys all memory of what you went into the video store to rent. Second, it destroys all memory of movies you have already rented. I can't tell you the number of times I have watched the opening scene of ducks waddling in a muddy rut and thought, *Dang, I've already seen* Cold Comfort Farm. O.K., four.

In addition to the filmic amnesia caused by the L'Arche de Video, I can forget a movie I've just seen in my local cineplex faster than Al Gore can switch his position on litmus tests. The lights go up, and it starts. By the time I reach the exit, a friend could say, "When he found that horse's head in the bed . . ." and I'm left stammering, "He did?!"

I can be cued back through patient prompting, but it takes me a while, and it might not last. Fortunately, a kind friend has turned me on to the online Internet Movie Database, and all my questions are more than answered. I only wish they'd post head shots with actors' names.

Despite obsessively micromanaging my mental health— ginseng and vitamin E, when I remember—these filmic lapses have never panicked me. In fact, they have seemed oddly familiar, albeit uncomfortable, for they are my youth.

While clearing boxes out of my Dad's attic, I came across a high school yearbook picture of me as queen of the Sweetheart Dance. The recently crowned king of the Sweetheart Dance, my date (?), was pinning a corsage to my not-at-all-heaving bosom.

What I remember of that night was my searing resentment of Tony Morgillo slow-dancing with Ruby Gill, a girl I mooned over most of my high school years. She was an unapologetic intellect, a stealth troublemaker, with jet-black hair and dreamy porcelain skin. She was a smart-ass cheerleader. Once, when the score of our pathetic boys' basketball game was 80–40, she started chanting, "Break that tie! Break that tie!" A wit like that, yet the team captain— Tony Morgillo, "the gorilla"—was the one who got to slow-dance with her. It should have been me.

My closeted youth was like a continuous lesbian film festival but with all the movies looped in some language I didn't speak. The hetero world outside sailed by, but it never really connected. Consequently I have little memory of many of its actual characters, conflicts, crises, resolutions.

Going to movies was a respite from my adolescence, but

it too was often an altered experience. Julie Andrews was the Ruby Gill of film. In *The Sound of Music,* when Baron von Christopher Plummer was in the rainy-night gazebo finally about to kiss Julie/Maria, it was me. And I was not singing, "Perhaps I had a wicked childhood, perhaps I had a miserable youth . . ." I was fixing to lay a big one on her.

Do I regret the lost memories? Yes. Do I regret how well I learned not to be in my own life? Yes, even today.

But regret gives way to new wonder. It is enormously cheering to me that there is a burgeoning gay and lesbian youth movement in high schools helping kids to find each other and, upon finding each other, to insist that they be active players in their own intricate, particular lives. Their sense of entitlement is bracing. Their memories are full.

And I remain flabbergasted that a movie like *Boys Don't Cry* ever got made and gains momentum, from Golden Globes to Oscar nods, even though it explores in minute detail the life of a young man, born a biological woman, who must become an actor in the movie of his life.

It is an excruciating, triumphant movie that collapses the boundaries between life and fantasy. Perhaps because it dares to deal in such an ordinary Midwestern way with an actual young life, I remember every scene, every detail, every character even at a month's distance from seeing it.

And I even remember the adenoidally challenged, open-mouthed popcorn eater who sat behind me.

(2000)

BUSH FATIGUE

I TOLD A FRIEND OF mine that if the unthinkable happened and W was elected, I was going to let my hair grow. She said, "Oh great, two really unpleasant things." Then the Bush Restoration hardware malfunctioned in Florida. With a premature triumphalism, they had already printed the inauguration invitations—BLACK TIE AND CHADOR— and were planning a 21,000-gun salute from the NRA. But then came the recount, and at press time they're still counting.

So what to do now? I am undecided. Should I go for a middle part and grow it long on the left, short on the right? Or should I get the much maligned but classic achy breaky lesbian split-level haircut, short on the top and sides, long in the back, in acknowledgment of the Nader vote?

I've got Bush fatigue. Not the good kind. It's causing me to think shallow follicular thoughts. Also I have not stopped eating since the night of the election. We've had so many highs and lows, Gore blues and Bush reds, blather and Rather. Until we can make up our minds, I'm sticking to Chee-tos for that undecided yellow.

Luckily, a few days after the vote, I attended the thirteenth annual Creating Change conference in Georgia, a red state. Sponsored by the National Gay and Lesbian Task Force. It is a raucous caucus of 2,000 gay, lesbian, transgendered, bisexual, old, young, multiracial grassroots activists from all over the country. I needed it.

At one session, the new executive director of the task force, Elizabeth Toledo, urged attendees to practice daily acts of rebellion and suggested letter writing, street protest, and volunteering in gay organizations. Then Florida organizer Nadine Smith invited everyone to a quickly convened election protest in Atlanta's Centennial Olympic Park. After months of impotent E-protesting, it was good to get out of the chat rooms into the streets and listen to labor organizers ("If this were a union vote, we'd all be in jail"), old civil rights workers ("A ballot is a person—we will not be denied"), and activist ("If this election bushwacking were happening in any other country, we'd be calling in U.N. election observers").

The conference inspired me to do more than hair care. I am going to work on election reform. In England, a country George Bush has never visited, campaigns are never longer than six weeks. If we did that here, there would be less need for truckloads of soft money. Forget Election

Day. We should make the first weekend in November Election Weekend. Since Americans will bet on anything, we could call it Off Track Voting. Mater of fact, make the ballots scratch tickets.

I am also going to work for term limits on pundits. It seemed that the early-morning rush to election judgment was because our high-paid commentariat was getting Bushed. Excuse us! I will push for the Olympic delay—no election results can be announced until 15 hours after the polls close. I also favor the French notion of *parité*—that is, pundits in proportion to the population. I cannot go through another campaign with mostly white boys talking with other white boys about other white boys. That includes the new darlings Russert, O'Reilly, and Matthews, who actually said that my "sister-in-law," the new junior senator from New York, Hillary Clinton, won on the victim vote.

Finally and preemptively, I have formed the Permanent Standing Committee to Impeach Bush (PSCTIB™). As with the Permanent Republication Committee of Sore Losers to Impeach Clinton, who believe the presidency is their own government entitlement program and are still steamed by the impertinent election of Bill Clinton, the aim of PSCTIB™ is simple: dogged, nagging contrarianism. We will start small. Send us any scurrilous personal W details, unverified Bush brushes, cockamamie (no insult to Mamie Eisenhower intended) conspiracy theories, rumors, and innuendos, and we will assign our relentless Starr-quality investigator to verify your claim weeks after we publish it.

Meanwhile, let's see this crisis as an opportunity. Imagine the possibilities of a "Bush and Dick" administration. We're on comedy cruise control for the next four years!

(2000)

My Passage to India

IN FEBRUARY I WENT WITH four friends to India. No, we were not President Clinton's advance team. My partner of thirteen years, Urvashi Vaid, whom I can't marry, and wouldn't if I could, even though we could use some new Corningware with matching tops, is Indian and we wanted to see from whence she came.

Since our return, I have been reduced to loopy, halting responses to the innocent query, "Soooo? Howazzit?" Perhaps the lingering effects of killer jet lag made me think I could cogently summarize my trip in this space. There already is a whole body of bad work from people sporting dressy bindis, inhaling bidis, strumming sitars, trying to convey their transformations through a haze of sandalwood incense.

So, think of the following as a mercifully short impressionistic slide show, in no particular order. Lights, please.

1. In Bombay, a city of sixteen million, [stop, review— that's twice New York City's population and there's no neat freak, anal retentive, control queen for mayor, and I wouldn't wish him on Bombay] we were stuck in one of the grimiest, noisiest, hottest traffic jams I have ever, ever endured. I had my very own claustrophobic passage-to-India moment, exited my body, and transported myself to the sweet spring air of a walk on the jetty in Provincetown. It is not that I am some highly evolved spiritual practitioner. It was pure survival or psychotic break.

2. When I was packing for our trip, I thought I would bring some cornball Valentines for my traveling companions, but then quickly forgot about it. Not to worry. In the past ten years, Hallmark has made its mark in India. Any variation of heartshaped schlock was up for bargaining in tiny stalls. India was an easy mark for Eros' arrows with its long tradition of over the top, swoony romantic movie musicals, cranked out by Bollywood. The romance still centers on arranged marriage, but that proved no consolation to the Hindu Fundamentalist goondas who trashed heart-festooned stalls and attacked romantic-looking couples on Valentine's Day. Roses are red, violets are blue, that Western love thing, here is taboo.

3. At least twice a day, whether we were in the city or the country, at little stalls or cantonment hotels, on planes or in rickshaws, I was "sirred." With short hair, no sari and minimal bangles, I was addressed "Sir" more times than a character in Peanuts. When one of my fellow travelers wore

the silver ankle bracelet we gave him, he stopped traffic in Kerala. One guide book said there are no gay men in India, just "frustrated husbands whose wives won't give them blow jobs." In the south, there has been a string of deaths of lesbian couples. The police report them as suicide pacts. Lesbians we met believed they were murders but had been stymied in their inquiries by the families of the women and the police.

4. For the three weeks of our visit, Deepa Mehta was all over the news. Fundamentalists shut down her movie set in Benares where she was trying to film *Water,* a movie about the treatment of Indian widows. Every story had to mention her earlier blasphemy, *Fire,* the story of two Indian women who fall in love. [See above. Not a Bollywood sanctioned theme.] In Bombay the ratio of men to women is 65 percent to 35 percent, due to amniocentesis, starvation, neglect. One guide responded to my frown with, "Why would you want to have a girl?"

5. Did I already show this slide? There are a lot of people in India. One billion of them. One sixth of the world's population. There's 719 people per square mile. Like fingerprints and snowflakes, I never saw two matching saris. I never saw one large piece of equipment either. India was scrambling to get the place ready for the other Clinton's visit. People were doing the most intensely physical, non-ergonomic, repetitive, carpal tunnel syndrome—inducing, OSHA "Don'ts" work. And if someone fell from the hand-tied bamboo scaffolding four stories up, there were always replacements.

6. We returned to Al Gore and George W fighting over Jesus Christ for their personal savior and running mate;

Who Wants to Marry A Multimillionaire? the ABC's of arranged marriage; California's passage of its Pre-emptive Prejudice Initiative on how marriage should be arranged; Oscar hoopla over the gender-bending *Boys Don't Cry*; the continued vilification of Hillary Clinton, not Swank; John McCain's suicide bomber attack on Fundamentalists in South Carolina.

Lights up, please.

In India, the function of religion as social enforcer, and of romance as the beautiful buttress of relentless heterosexuality with its rigid gender roles are perhaps more obvious hallmarks of patriarchy and its oppression of women than in the United States. Because of that, nothing at home looks the same. For that, thank you, India.

(2000)

THE FIREFIGHTER
NEXT DOOR

ON MONDAY NIGHT, SEPTEMBER 10, we finally had our across-the-hall neighbors, Kevin and Jen, over for dinner.

Jen had recently quit her job with MTV International and was home more. A year ago, they bought two apartments across from us, and when he wasn't working as a fireman, Kevin was doing most of the construction to combine them. Whenever there was some problem in our place, I'd ask him over to look at it. He'd look, nod, and invariably say, "I gotta guy."

Over dinner, I asked Kevin how he came to be a fireman. He told a long story of all the jobs he'd had, interrupted by Jen kicking him under the table, teasing him about rambling. I loved both the looping narrative and their familiarity with each other. Later, when they got back to their apartment, she told him he was starting to tell Aunt Patty stories.

On Tuesday morning, Kevin reported for the 9:00 A.M. shift. The call came from the World Trade Center at 9:05. His ladder company was out of the firehouse at 9:08. That night, we went down to sit with Jen at the firehouse as she met firemen returning for a shower and a three-hour nap. She said that the fire department is very strict about making the fighters take a break. When Kevin was not in the first wave of returnees, she knew his storied luck had run out. Our "I-gotta-guy" guy did not come back.

The next days were a blur of locating friends and family, hearing stories, watching television, feeling nauseous, and cooking. We invited people over for Saturday night dinner, just to do something, to be together. Our one-bedroom, upper West Side apartment is small, but we squeezed in fifteen for dinner and opened our doors to Kevin and Jen's large family across the hall. We wandered back and forth. I met Aunt Patty.

Just as people were arriving for dinner, we got a call from a friend who lives downtown. After a quick check-in, she said that people were meeting on Sunday night to discuss what to do. I said we'd be there. My girlfriend was shocked because, unlike her, I am not a group person. If there are more than twenty-five people in a room, I would rather grab a microphone, move us out in an hour, and get paid.

Sunday night, with just a few initial phone calls, fifty people showed up. I generally have no patience with going around the room, saying your name and a few self-identifying sentences. Process is for cheese. But as each person took her turn, my resistance wore down, and the fear and despair of the week began to recede.

Then longtime New York activist Jessica Neuwirth read the petition she'd written, called "New Yorkers Say No to War" (www.petitiononline.com/notowar/petition.html). Out of that petition, we decided to start a group. Then followed hours of discussion about what to call ourselves. Was it better to use a peace frame, or was it more effective to use a security frame? There was that "let-me-be-the-devil's-advocate" fellow I loathe, who kept bringing up important points.

We decided to meet again the following Tuesday night. I surprised myself and volunteered to be on the committee to help set the next meeting's agenda. We met for two more hours. Among us were exhausted activists who had finally returned from the racism conference in South Africa, cagey former Act-Uppers, and *Vagina Monologue*-ists. I have renewed admiration for my girlfriend's twenty-five years of such meetings.

We gathered again, more of us, with news of what else was happening in the city. We got reports from attorneys specializing in international law and from folks at the United Nations. After more discussion of the inclusiveness of the petition (Should it specifically include Afghan women? Should it mention the death penalty?), we broke into committees: arts, fundraising, actions, media, connectivity. We reported back. We scheduled the next meeting.

After each long session, I went out to dinner with a cadre of friends, hungry for their sweet faces and no longer willing to accept that New Yorkers are just too busy to get together.

Late each night, when my girlfriend and I returned from our peace meals, we would see huge piles of shoes outside Kevin and Jen's apartment. We would knock, open the unlocked door, and walk in to see their relatives all crammed in, looking grim and spent. They were all in stockinged feet, to honor Kevin's newly polished parquet floors.

Slowly, the reports changed from "still no news" to "we haven't given up hope" to "we gave them DNA samples."

In the days since, I've thought of telling Jen about our work, but each time her grief has stopped me, and I don't want to do anything that might close the doors between our apartments.

(2001)

Bless You, Father

On the evening of October 5, my dad died in Syracuse, N.Y. He was 92 years old. After a fall this summer he went to the hospital and from there was admitted to a nursing home. His health had been failing for a long time and the five of us kids were committed to keeping him in his home, the home we grew up in, as long as we could and to caring for him as well as he cared for my mother during the ten years she suffered from Parkinson's.

My two brothers and their wives, who live in Syracuse, gracefully managed an intricate schedule of doctor visits, house upkeep, and day and night caregivers, mostly women they found through his beloved Catholic parish, where he had been a daily communicant, a lector, and offering collector.

We out-of-town children made regular visits home to

relieve the hometown kin and of course to spend time with Dad. He was elegant, gentlemanly. Even at his frailest and with increasing senile dementia, he would try to rise when we came home and would always ask, "What can I get for you?"

I'm shocked that I can't call him and just talk about the weather, but I am enormously relieved that we had no unfinished business when he died. Even though we did not discuss my lesbianism, much less his heterosexuality in great detail, there was the possibility of honesty because I had come out to him.

It is a regret I still have about my mom. By the time I was confident enough in my lesbianism to come out to my mother, it did not seem fair. I knew we would fight, and advanced Parkinson's had left her unable to talk. She loved Richard Nixon, hated Betty Friedan, and was a fiercely conservative, devout Catholic, who once got out of her wheelchair to turn off the TV because, "that Phil Donohue was talking about orgasms like they were three for a nickel."

She and my father were high school sweethearts who delayed their wedding for a decade because of the Depression and then World War II. They were married for forty-two years. She ruled her family of five children with the velvet hammer of "Wait until your father gets home." At home he was stern, fair, and I never doubted that he loved me.

For a long time after I came out to my brothers and sisters, we abided by a tacit conspiracy, "Don't tell Dad, it could kill him." Finally thanks to the patient prodding of my girlfriend, the sheer force of the gay movement and, quite frankly, the possibility that he might see me on television with "openly lesbian comic" in quotes under my head, I decided to test my notion of unconditional paternal love. Some time after my Mom died, I came out to my father in a letter.

He called me two days later and immediately said that he loved me, that he knew I was a feminist, but hadn't known that I was a lesbian. All he wanted was for me to be happy and safe and to get health insurance. Turns out he had a very wide libertarian streak that he did not or could not show when my Mother was alive.

It was a pleasure to introduce him to more of my life, my friends, my work without vague pronouns. Once when he was visiting us in Provincetown, after we had walked Commercial Street in high season, we had some friends over for dinner to meet him. The only conversational rule I laid down ahead of time was no discussion of sex toys. That was for my benefit.

My father looked like an older Paul Newman most of his later years. In his youth he was an acclaimed athlete with thick jet black hair, and a great body. During dinner I got out some old pictures of him in his football uniform, and passed them around. One of my gay men friends looked at the picture and spontaneously kvelled, "Oh, Mr. Clinton, you're so humpy." My friend was mortified. My father smiled. I think he was flattered.

The dinner conversation ranged heatedly through gay politics, gay theory, gay gossip. Toward the end, my dear girlfriend asked, "Well, Mr. Clinton, (he was very formal; I might have called him Mr. Clinton a couple of times) what do you think we as gay people can do to make more bridges to straight people?"

My father did one of his patented, exquisitely timed pauses and replied, "Keep talking."

In his memory, I think I will.

(2003)

MAD VOW DISEASE

. . .

That old kidder, Kafka, described marriage: "A cage went in search of a bird."
From gay liberation, to gay marriage. It's come to this. Les Cages aux Folles.
Though I prefer to live in sin, I defend the right to get gay married. Not W,
The Lord of the Wedding Rings. He believes gays are weapons of marriage
destruction. Methinks he doth protest too much. There is no proof. Give the
marriage inspectors more time to do their jobs. Despite a Defense of Marriage Act, state laws, a culture of hetero-romance, a get-out-the-vote
strategy disguised as a proposed constitutional amendment, covenant mar-
riages, and a huge Marriage Industrial Complex, wedlockdown success rate
is only 50 percent. It is just not going well for straight people. I'm concerned.
If they really want to protect marriage, they should call in the ATF.
Without infrastructure or incentive, gay relationships go on. We are weapons
of mass affection.

Freedom Not to Marry Kit

RECENTLY, I WAS READING ONE of the many glossy gay magazines I get. There's a sentence you never used to hear. No more plain brown wrappers for us! The only magazine I insist come under wraps into my neighborhood is *The New Republic.*

Now, all manner of gay magazines with "out" in the title are mailed openly to post office boxes all over the country. *Out and About*—gay travel. *Trout*—gay sports trolling. *Doubt*—a magazine for bisexuals. *Pout*—The Log Cabin newsletter (great article about Bob Dole returning gay money).

And O.K., I wasn't really reading. I was looking at the pictures! Famous gay people. Famous dead suspected gay people. Famous gay half-sisters playing ministers at gay weddings on hip, gay-friendly shows. Gay cruises to take.

Gay things to buy. In between the ad for gay real estate and gay colonies ("Swallow a prism, shit a rainbow!"), I spotted an ad for "The Freedom to Marry Kit." Of course, I wondered, "Who is Kit? And why do we want to marry her? Or him?"

It was a very androgynous "Ask Pat" moment. I could understand the Freedom to Marry Melissa. Or the Freedom to Marry Martina, with the very clear, signed prenuptial agreements, of course, but this Kit thing had me mystified.

Turns out the FTM kit is designed to help concerned gays organize their municipalities for the freedom to marry! Now if I were into handicapping, sorry, predicting the next issue for gay people to get het up about, it would not have been gay marriage.

I would have though our issue would be violence against gays—witness the murder in Oregon of two known lesbian activists. Investigators think the motive was robbery. Like rainbow-colored freedom rings are hard to come by.

Or I would have predicted we would be organizing around the Supreme Court's upcoming ruling on the Colorado amendment, or at least having a small action to protest that the Clinton Administration did not even see fit to file an amicus brief.

I would have thought we would have been out in the streets over health care, given the cost of caring for people living with AIDS and the disproportionately high rates of breast cancer among lesbians.

But no, the issue du anno burbling up in the gay movement is the Freedom to Marry. Go figure.

I have applied rigorous self-criticism to understand why this issue does not exactly knock the dots off my dice. It's not the first time I have had to work up enthusiasm for a gay issue.

Gays in the military was a challenge. Instead of thinking that I was enthusing about gay guys convincing their dads that they were man enough to kill other men, I got there by thinking of it as a jobs program. Not full steam. Think vaporizer.

I have examined my reluctance to hop on the gay bandwagon with the "Just Married" sign and tin can tails rattling up the street. Of course I believe that gay people should have the right to marry, and have equal access to all benefits accruing to straight married people, but for myself, I prefer living in sin.

The freedom not to marry was always one of the things I enjoyed about being gay. So was the freedom not to have children. Because so many gay people are having children—they definitely have that thrill-seeking gene—it follows that they would want the civil protections of marriage for those children.

Don't get me wrong. I will take anything that gets new gay people incensed, interested, involved in the gay movement. I'm just having a very Peggy "Is That All There Is?" Lee moment.

It's hard to be gay and a people pleaser. This FTM minimovement seems to be fueled by a desire to show that we can be upstanding citizens, with children, and that we will keep sex within the confines of marriage. As if.

Instead of spending time on the freedom to marry, I

think we should try to talk straight people out of getting married. It's not going well for them: Enid/Joe; Nicole/O.J.; Di/Chuck/Camilla; Lisa Marie/Michael. This would certainly cut down on a whole range of civil-service jobs. See, I'm doing my best to balance the budget.

If there had been this freedom to marry when I was a child, would it have meant that I would not have had to hide crushes? If it meant that I could go home and say to my Irish-Catholic mother, "Oh, Mom, I just met the most dreamy girl! I asked her to an Earth, Wind, and Fire concert and she said yes!" And my mother would joyfully say, "Oh, honey, that's wonderful. What do you love about her? Will you practice safe sex? Oh, no. Wait, you can't until you are married."

If, big if, that is the net trickle-down effect of the Freedom to Marry movement, I'll stop saying "marred" instead of "married" as soon as I get my multicolored FTM card. I've got to register my china pattern: gold-leaf entwined women's symbols on a purple background.

(1996)

Veiled Threats

On May 15, 2002, six members of the House of Representatives introduced a proposed constitutional amendment that says, "Marriage shall consist only of the union of a man and a woman." Don't throw your rice pudding at me until I finish telling you why I'm all for this prenuptial agreement. Hint: my "We Don't Want Your Stinkin' Marriage" campaign never caught on.

Why this proposed amendment now, you might ask? Or you might not, depending on your level of distraction from unspecified warnings of possible attacks, or possible warnings of unspecified attacks. My Google search engine, usually so chipper and self-congratulatory about the time it takes to find stuff for me, seems to be in orange "Apocalypse Pretty Soon" threat level and is "preparing to work at an alternate site." For some reason, it won't cough up the info I seek, but I bet those six House members need some fast campaign cash.

The lead sponsor of the measure, Rep. Ronnie Shows, [D-Miss.] says that the amendment is necessary to protect the sanctity of marriage and that "the overwhelming consensus among Americans is that we must not allow the institution of marriage to be degraded."

As if!

As if heterosexuals all by themselves were not completely capable of degrading marriage through divorce, pricey annulments, child abuse, domestic violence. Straight people have been doing the aerial bombing of marriage for quite some time. Now gay people are the robot drones sent in to do the hand-to-hand combat and mop up operations in the Canna caves?

As if homosexuals were that powerful. Although, come to think of it, we have been recently credited with the destruction of the U.S. Catholic Church through bouts of "ecclesiastic flamboyance." Sidebar: you just wish sometimes that the Church protected children as much as they protect fetuses.

Add to our degradation of same-old-sex marriage, our devastation of the military and it should become clear to someone—hullo, Donald Rumsfeld—that we are an underused weapon of capital M and small m, mass destruction. We're a veritable Triple Crown: The Priestness, The Breeder's Cup, The Kandahar Derby.

Discussions of the amendment are dryly juridical, all full faith and credit, state's rights, and federalist principles. Bob Barr who sponsored the Defense of Marriage Act (DOMA) said the amendment goes too far because it violates the principle of states' rights. Bob Barr accusing someone of going too far! Fire up those Giggle Search engines! Ari Fleischer said, "All I know is that it's already the law of the land, signed by Bill Clinton. The president supports the law of the land in this case." In other cases, he pretty much does whatever he wants, Ari did not add.

Christopher Andres, of the ACLU, perhaps succumbing hyperbolic atmosphere of our time, [see tortured 'Canna cave' reference above], called the proposed amendment "the legal equivalent of a nuclear bomb." Others have called it "The American Gothic Amendment," calling to mind either the famous farm couple aesthetic or Dick and Lon Cheney's last Christmas card.

To me it's Anita Bryant, but bigger. It's Lane Bryant. Anita's "Save the Children" campaign which always sounded like a set aside program, mobilized a whole generation of gay activists. But in a narrow way. We've become too comfortably single-issued to get riled up about the end-of-welfare-as-we-know-it law which would punish the poor while rewarding heterosexual marriage. We barely paid attention past the grudging posthumous salutes to gay heroes of September 11, to the ongoing story of denial of benefit claims to surviving gay and unmarried straight partners. We think the priestly marriage issue is separate from us. We are bought off, bought in, assimilated, living ma vida en rose loca in white, affluent gay-ted communities with our very own gay channels.

The last thing we need is another fight about gay marriage, but bring it on. Anything to get people engaged. As for me, I prefer to live in sin.

(2002)

Mad Vow Disease

FYI: The Summer of Gay has been extended into the
Year of the Queer. Another heads up: Mad Vow Disease,
once limited to wholesome, unimpeachable gay couples
earnestly seeking to take on the rights and responsibilities
of marriage, has jumped the pen and crossed into the general population. There the unfortunate symptoms are
frothing apocalypticism, fractured reasoning, knee jerking,
and involuntary eye rolling. It ain't pretty.

After the Massachusetts Supreme Court ruling that the
Constitution did not ban gay marriage, it was likened to
moral chaos, nuclear war, partial birth abortion, and the
extinction of the human race by Bill Bennett, Gary Bauer,
the Focus on other People's Family, the frowning Concerned Women, and others. The Red Sox "Curse of the

Bambino" was not mentioned. They all seemed to be doing variations on the talking points memo circulated by Wedge-master Karl Rove.

Columnist David Brooks opined in his *New York Times* column that marriage makes "us better than we deserve to be." I was with him until he said that marriage at its best allows couples to say to each other: "Love you? I AM you." Is it just me, or is that really creepy? He said that gays should not be denied this "opportunity," and that "we should insist on gay marriage." Holy codependent crisis, Brooksman! Thanks, but no thanks on the forced nuptialization.

The media, when they weren't giving the O.J. treatment to Michael Jackson, were parroting more Rove power points. They announced that the issue of gay marriage was going to be a big problem for the Democratic presidential candidates. Following their script, many Dems acted as if it were and did nothing to clear up the murk. Their campaigns announced that, and I'm conflating wildly here, they were not in favor of gay marriage, despite having gay relatives, but they were in favor of civil unions and they hated that little upstart Confederate flag-waving front-running Vermont governor for bringing the whole thing up in the first place. Don't ask, don't tell. Want to see my prescription drug plan?

There were some bright spots. When Jerry "onemanonewoman.com" Falwell faced off against Barney Frank on CNN, he conceded, "I'm not in favor of putting people in jail for what they do in their bedrooms." He had been just a few months ago, but Lawrence v. Texas must have converted him. Polls found that while people generally were more favorable toward gays, gay marriage gave them the heebie-jeebies. Hold that first thought. People are more favorable to gays!? Progress has been made!

The problem with all the convoluted, trying to have it both ways, hair-splitting arguments against gay marriage is that it involves people. How inconvenient.

In the midst of all this marriage mishegoss, one of my best friends was dealing with the sad-beyond-sad details of the death of her partner of twenty-seven years, a woman who thought marriage was an abomination and who often joked that "married" is "marred" with an I.

The day my inbox overflowed with messages about the Massachusetts decision, I received two e-mails from my friend. In her morning note, she told me she had just gotten a call from Human Resources at the university where they both taught. They were holding her partner's last pay-check and needed an affidavit from a RECOGNIZED (her caps) next of kin to release it.

That afternoon, she e-mailed me that New York State laws say that even if someone has filed a will, you have to send a letter requesting a waiver of contest of will to next of kin. That meant, in this case, to her partner's mother, who had fought with my friend over care and do-not-resuscitate orders during her partner's yearlong battle with a brain tumor.

Apparently, we do need a piece of paper from the City Hall. Not to keep us tried and true. But to claim our due.

(2003)

Wedded to the Republicans

THESE ARE HARD DAYS FOR Gay Republicans. When the Lord of the Wedding Rings held his no-questions-asked press conference, he said he was sorely "troubled." Finally an admission! But no, he said he was troubled by what was happening in Massachusetts (those Salem witch trials are over), in California (many little gaybies are being named "Gavin"), and by activist judges overruling the will of the people, (okay to select him as president, but otherwise, big no-no).

In his grim-faced version of the Charlton Heston, Bush essentially said, "They'll have to pry this wedding ring from my cold dead hand." His straight plan for the gay man and lesbian was to endorse a constitutional amendment defining marriage as a union of a man and a woman. Why an amendment when a simple Post-it will do?

For Gay Republicans—and one-third of gay voters in the last presidential election voted Republican—this is a very perverse Sally Field moment: "You hate me! You hate me! You really, really hate me!" They have been publicly dissed, discounted, and double-crossed. And still some remain wedded to the Republican Party. What some call denial, others call pragmatism.

After a show in North Carolina, I was sitting at dinner next to a young lesbian couple. I asked one of the women what she did, and she said, "Make trouble." During the next course, she came out to me as a Republican.

She was from a long line of Democrats and Baptist fundamentalists, and for those of you who were wondering, it's easier to break away from the Democrats than from the Baptists. I asked her if she would not bolt her party because of the proposed amendment. She said that she felt it was important to stay in the party, that if people like her left, all that would remain would be religious extremists. She said she was discouraged by the anti-gay marriage amendment but felt energized to reclaim her party. I admired her willingness to be in the fray and in their faces and suggested that for making trouble nothing would beat getting active in her party and then going in the voting booth and vote for John Kerry. She laughed and clapped me a good one on the back.

With all the focus on gay marriage (and I hope someone, somewhere in a gender studies seminar is figuring out why two-thirds of the gay couples getting married are lesbian), little attention is being paid to single gay people. If you're single and gay, you're really isolated today. I asked a gay friend who is single about this at a rally, and he told me—while carrying his "Whose Constitution? Our Constitution!" sign—that he felt a nagging resentment that he couldn't join in any rainbow games.

Then there are those gays and lesbians who believe that marriage is a dead-end for the sexual liberation movement. Why, they ask, should we demand to join an institution that is so confining and conservative? I sympathize with this view.

But I also agree with the argument that gays and lesbians should have all the rights that heterosexuals do. The daily insults from the slippery slopeheads are not only offensive, they also fuel an increase in anti-gay violence and grave and growing internalized homophobia. Brooklyn Bishop Nicholas DeMarzio, which is Italian for "from Mars," bloviated that if we allow gays to marry, the next thing you know people will want to marry their pets.

Trust me, for most gay people, our next thought after popping the question is not, "And if you won't have me, I'll marry the cat."

Our next thought is, "For this we pay taxes?"

(2004)

Miss Marriage Suggests

ACCORDING TO THE LATEST REPORTS from my Weapons of Marriage Destruction inspectors, civilization as we know it is still as steady as she goes. That's either the good or the bad news.

In my own on-the-ground observation, my siblings and their partners seem to be holding steady. Ditto my straight friends. Once on an express subway, I did sense that a couple sitting across from my partner and me were in some distress, but I could not be sure if our proximity was the cause.

Although J-Lo is on her third husband, there has been no noticeable spike in polygamy. Last I checked, even the Mormon governor of Massachusetts, Mitt Mitt full of shit Romney had not taken on any extra wives.

Each Sunday I scan *The New York Times* Vows section and so far have not espied pictures of anyone smiling cheek to jowl with a pet. Additionally, there have been no reports of a surge in gift registration at PetCo. Rice, not Kibbles 'n Bits, is still thrown.

Except for one unfortunate nuptial where an attempt was made to throw Condoleezza Rice, ceremonies have been, by all accounts, very well-behaved. Sigh. However, in personal and sub-contracted field research on the civil effect of gay marriage, there are repeated references to extreme social discomfort, again, that mad vow dis-ease. This is to be expected in times of what, for some, is rapid cultural change.

I would like to propose some general etiquette suggestions to smooth out the cultural unsteadiness we are all enduring. It's also a chance for me to use really stilted passive voice and that nifty etiquettish "we" that Miss Manners and others get to use.

First, it is always preferable to preface the pressure-packed "Didja get married?" with an initial "Hello." or "How are you?" or even a "How about those Red Sox?" We are amused to observe how our questions have changed—from "Who's your daddy?" of early gay liberation, to "Who's the father?" of the baby boom; from the propositional "Do you wanna?" to the proposing "Do you wanna get married?"

Second, such a well-meaning but intrusive question often provoke conversations for which we have not been prepared. In the inevitable back and forth that follows, we recommend couples not use the following lines: "Let's wait until we can do it in New York State," "Let's wait until your mother dies," or "If you really loved me, you'd be down on your good knee right now."

Third, a word about hyphenates. If your last name is already hyphenated from your feminist-progressive childhood and you marry a similarly hyphenated other, for the sake of your friends and the cake decorator, we encourage you to drop or combine names. But if, say, a Lyon-Bush marries a Canby-Beaton, by all means keep it and quickly publish those vows.

Fourth, wordlessly waving your newly beringed fingered hand like a flopping desperate fish in another's face is declassé. We are so unaccustomed to admiring each other's wedding rings, the wildly flailing hand suggests not nuptials but a worrisome tremor of near papal proportions. While we're on that topic, it's vulgar to set up that papal wave bye-bye pool unless it's for a fundraiser for a very good cause [see five below]. Especially if you ever want to receive the Eucharist in your parish again.

Fifth, while it always lovely to receive gifts, we recommend that your wedding registry be a list of national GLBT organizations where your well-wishers can send donations in your name so those groups can continue to fight the inevitable anti-gay marriage initiatives.

Sixth, in all of the above, we encourage everyone to be a little bit more sensitive to single gay people.

Seventh, we would be remiss if we did not clarify for the questioning that if you think you are gay and don't want to get married, you could still be gay.

(2004)

AFTERWORD

.   .   .

In 1970, I earned a Masters in English. It was pre-Women's Studies. Yes, dears, there was such a time. In 1978–1979, I attended The Women's Writer Center in Cazenovia, New York, and finally began to read the women I had craved. I thought my head would blow up. Since it was the Writer's Center, I also wrote. I wanted to write humor but, given my delaying, self-justifying, Jesuitical mind, I felt I should first research women's humor. I refined my question about humor with each visiting teacher—Rita Mae Brown, Olga Broumas, Marge Piercy—so that when the poet, Adrienne Rich, finally arrived, I puffed myself up and began, "There doesn't seem to be much written about feminist humor and. . . ." Adrienne stopped my paragraph of a question and asked, "Why don't you write it?" When Adrienne Rich asks you to do something, you do it.

Making Light: Another Dimension

IMAGINE A TABLE. A ROUND one. Women sitting around it. Some leaning up on forearms. Some leaning forward, resting china on palms, listening. There are candles lit. They light up the circle of faces. They are all women. Six or seven. The remains of a dinner are on the table. Coffee cups, wine glasses. Someone forgot to clear off the butter dish.

The sound is of talking—one woman, then another, sometimes two or three at a time. And they are laughing, tears streaming down their faces. Tears glistening in the candlelight. They are gasping and moaning and rocking back and forth. One woman tips back in her chair, pushes back, elbows locked, she laughs head back and the candles light up the triangle of her chin.

I want to talk of women laughing and women's humor. I want to say that our humor can illuminate our oppression so that we can overcome it. I want to talk of those cherished hilarious moments of women laughing together as coming from the same source as the erotic. I want to talk of women laughing together as an intimation of women in community. And I wish I could speak of all these things at the same time.

Old voices taunt me as I begin. "I cannot tell when you are being serious and when you are being funny." "When are you going to get serious?" My own voice asks me, "If humor is such a powerful teaching device, why are you so serious now? Writing with such a furrowed brow? Scowling as you type?"

Those voices speak from an old separation: The old dichotomy between serious and humorous. An ancient dichotomy, one of many. Serious is more real. Serious is truth. Humorous is less than real, trivial, trifling. And humor is not quite truthful. There is no place for humor in the serious analysis of relationships or language or oppression. Humor is somehow off the mark, dodging the issue, masking and hiding from something more serious. All those voices ask questions which state, even in the asking, that there is a division between serious and humorous.

For most of my life, I have worked hard on my humor. I have always believed it is serious. Before coming out, I spent years covering, protecting that belief. I covered so well, I almost lost it. Early on, I learned to deny my wisecracks, to say I was just kidding. I learned to apologize for insights which flew unplanned and unbidden out of me. Later I learned to turn those wisecracks on myself and others, usually other women. I learned it was dangerous to make fun of men and I protected myself. For years I worked hard, building layer upon layer to protect myself and my humor. After I came out, I began working hard to strip away all those layers.

I must say that I have always loved women best because I have laughed best with them. For years I mourned deeply because I knew I was supposed to get married and I knew I would never be able to laugh with a man as I could laugh with a woman. I have always used a sort of intuitive laugh meter and no man ever measured up.

"After I came out"—I surprise myself with the ease I now have in describing that process. Women who were imagining a world where "coming out" is an obsolete and unnecessary process helped me. I heard Muriel Rukeyser read her poetry, the first woman I had ever heard read, and I heard her say to me in the calmest of voices not to be afraid and to "Pay attention to what they tell you to forget."[1] I read Mary Daly and I heard her say that the land of the fathers is the land of reversals and to pay attention.[2]

And there is a moment I count as the moment when I did come out. A very conscious pivotal moment when I said to myself, "It is all right. Come on. Why not?"

I met a woman and we laughed and made love and we laughed as we made love and we made love as we laughed. It was serious and I tell you I was happy. I told a friend about it. I told her I was so happy and why and she actually said to me, with a sneer: "Well, you've certainly made a commitment to joy in your life." And I almost denied it. But she was right. As a lesbian, I have made a commitment to joy in my life, and let me tell you, Joy is not an easy woman to please.

I have always been told not to make light. I say now I believe in making light. Light enough to see by. Light enough to fly free. Both have to do with this woman's movement. Without our humor, without making light, we become too heavy to move; it is impossible to see. A feminist humorist makes light. She is a fumerist, a sparking incendiary with blazes of light and insight. Fumerists make whys cracks. We ask our own questions and they have the potential of splitting the world apart. Light shines through the whys cracks we make and illuminates all aspects of our oppression.

Consider feminist humor and consider the lichen. Growing low and lowly on enormous rocks, secreting tiny amounts of acid, year after year, eating into the rock. Making places for water to gather, to freeze and crack the rock a bit. Making soil, making way for grasses to grow. Making way for rosehips and sea oats, for aspen and cedar. It is the lichen which begins the splitting apart of the rocks, the changing of the shoreline, the shape of the earth. Feminist humor is serious, and it is about the changing of this world.

It is about making light in this land of reversals, where we are told if we are laughing, tears streaming down our faces, that we have no sense of humor. Where men who tell jokes about women are funny and women who tell jokes about men are antimale. Where there is, year after year, the appearance of a cartoon depicting the same "funny" scene of a barelegged man in an old raincoat exposing himself to a woman. The cartoon is made even "funnier" by the horrified look on the woman's face. In this land of reversals, rape becomes one of the funniest, most "trivial" things a guy can do. The ultimately practical joke.

Men have used humor against women for so long—we know implicitly whose butt is the butt of their jokes—that we do not trust humor. Masculine humor is deflective. It allows denial of responsibility, the Oh-I-was-just-kidding disclaimer. It is escapist, something to gloss over and get through the hard times, without ever having to do any of the hard work of change. Masculine humor is essentially not about change. It is about the maintenance of the status quo. There is nothing new under the sons; they are always dead serious.

The work of fumerists is reclaiming and renaming our own humor. Unlike masculine humor, feminist humor is about exposure. It is about shedding light on our experience. It is an active ethic, not a passive acceptance of an imposed status quo. We fumerists say we are not staying in some happy holding pattern, passively waiting until it is over. We say we are going to laugh and by our laughing, change things. It is a very active ethic of withdrawing the seriousness of our beliefs from men's enterprises. We are saying that the joke is no longer on us. We say we are not going to die laughing at their stories anymore.

Feminist humor is not some tidy reversal, some "Take my husband, please." Nor is it some compendium of feminist jokes and anecdotes. It is a deeply radical analysis of the world and our being in the world because it, like the erotic, demands a commitment to joy. Feminist humor is a radical analysis because we are saying that we have the right to be happy, that we will not settle for less. Both our erotic sense and our sense of humor spring from what Audre Lorde calls a "capacity for joy."[3] My vision of feminist humor always expands when I read that essay and I have always known in my bones that the erotic and humor are connected. I count my first sensual memory from a very specific time while I was laughing wildly, hysterically, falling down on the ground laughing with my girl friends. It was a sensual feeling of gasping for air with women, making sounds we usually did not make, exhilarating, helpless, free, alive, wild, with soft moaning after. I knew it then. I still know it. I cherish the women I sleep with as I cherish the women I laugh with. It is a doubly strong bond, because I laugh with the women I sleep with; it is a doubly powerful participation in joy, a wonderful coming together.

Humor leads the way; it moves us past those inbred, ingrained resistances. We make light. We see where to go and we are light enough to move there. In a male culture which places all emphasis on the serious, we women sometimes feel we need to outserious the man. Not often enough then, in the midst of excruciating conversations, do I have the good sense to remember that the whole point of our talking is that we are both working to make room for more joy in our lives. That the point of a conversation with my lover is not that we stay in painful analysis of our resistance to the erotic, but that we move on. That we do not stay in the dead-ended, albeit comfortable and familiar corners that we have talked and talked ourselves into, but that we move on. Humor can move us, I know it. When I become so serious about myself, so heavy that I cannot move, I have to laugh. When I realize I am judging my life by some standard of male seriousness, I have to laugh to save myself. The whole world hates a happy woman and it does its best to keep us apart.

So many times, I have tried to describe some moment of laughter with women to another woman. I have fumbled and tried to tell who said what and to whom, feeling a certain frantic helplessness in the face of her patient quizzical interest. Inevitably, when I finish, the woman says, "And? . . ." And I am left saying, "Well, you really had to be there." Quite simply, there is no recapturing those moments for each other—you do have to be there. The demand for our presence in the moment is another way in which our sense of humor and the erotic are entwined. For full participation in the erotic, you have to be there. Both moments demand that we withdraw our energies from male enterprises, that we are present to ourselves and to each other.

These moments of women laughing are intimations of what we can be together in community. They suggest another dimension, where separations and divisions are bridged. I do not mean to suggest some other-worldly zone, some transcendent leap into another karmic dimension where all is happy and oh-so-wonderful. It is a very real place where, because we are present to ourselves, we are absent to the world of men; where we are thus present/absent at the same time. It is a utopic dimension in the here and now predicated on the sharing of joy.

If we say that feminist humor is basically about the sharing of joy, we listen to Audre Lorde again:

> *The sharing of joy, whether physical, emotional, psychic or intel-lectual, forms a bridge between sharers which can be the basis for understanding much of what is not shared between them and lessens the threat of their difference.* [4]

As Julia Penelope and Susan Robbins have explored in "Lesbian Humor," one of the characteristics of our humor is feminine bonding.[5] In the context of male humor, our humor has too often been used for female binding—we have told jokes on ourselves, we have "trivialized" our actions, we have not taken ourselves seriously as we have tried to keep each other in place.

A part of feminist humor is encouragement, expansion and movement. So often as a child I remember my parents and teachers saying, "Don't laugh, it only encourages her." The difference between the female binding of male humor and the feminist bonding of fumerists is that we are encouraging each other to be all that we can. By our laughing, we are encouraging each other to move, take off, fly free. In that sense we are participating in an ever-expanding, non-entropic source of biophilic energy.[6] Our moments of feminist humor, blazes of light and insight, are intimations of a deep, unconsumable source of energy that is within ourselves.

Gloria Kaufman in her introduction to *Pulling Our Own Strings* discusses "pick-ups" and expands the notion of encouragement. Pick-up humor is a "healthy contrast to mainstream humor, much of which seems to knock people down—or laugh at people who are already down. Laughs come from a perceived superiority of the hearer or reader to the character ridiculed. Pick-up humor is based on equity. Through it, we do not laugh at people, we bond with them." [7]

Male penile humor, the ultimate in stand-up comedy, is based on a hierarchical power structure of the put-down. Fumerists are more stand-with comediennes. Each of us is equal to the task of making light, shedding light on our experiences, encouraging each other to change and move. It is feminine bonding in an ever-expanding movement. Times of women laughing together, jamming words and ideas, riffing off each other, are times of lucid/ludic celebration and they are times of a natural equality which hint at the possibility of how equality can work in a community of women.

Classically, humor has depended on the existence of accepted norms. What is outside the norm is considered humorous. Women, as the quintessential outsiders, have always been funny, trivial to men. As Julia Penelope writes, "By definition we are outside, and the world we inhabit encompasses the paradox of Utopia, from the Greek 'eu topis' that which is nowhere (the no place) that which is everywhere (the all place)." [8] I have said that feminist humor and women laughing together are intimations of another, utopic dimension. By reclaiming our humor and using it to empower ourselves we are paradoxically serious and humorous at the same time. By being present to ourselves and thus absent to the world of men, we are present/absent at the same time. We are outsiders with an in-group bonding power based on the sharing of our common joy.

Do not imagine my old taunting voices have been still. They have been alternately shrilling, "Come on, get serious" and "You've got to be kidding." They have been telling me more and more loudly to stop this writing on humor. They have become so loud, I know I am on to something.

(1982)

NOTES

1 Muriel Rukeyser, "Double Ode," in *The Gates* (New York: McGraw Hill, 1976), p. 10.

2 Mary Daly. *Gyn/Ecology: The Metaethics of Radical Feminism* (Boston: Beacon Press, 1978), p. 8 and p. 79. See also exploration of "trivial," p. 79.

3 Audre Lorde, "Uses of the Erotic: The Erotic as Power" (Brooklyn: Out & Out Books, 1978), p. 5.

4 Ibid., p. 5.

5 Julia Penelope and Susan W. Robbins, "Lesbian Humor," *The Journal of Women's Liberation*, vol. 5, no. 1.

6 Daly, *Gyn/Ecology*, p. 373.

7 Gloria Kaufman and Mary Kay Blakely, *Pulling Our Own Strings: Feminist Humor and Satire* (Bloomington: Indiana University Press, 1980), p. 16.

8 Julia Penelope, "Uninhabited Angels: Metaphors for Love," paper presented at NCTE conference, Kansas City, Mo., November 1978.